To: Lillian

May the Lord bless everything your hand touches!

PRAISE FROM INFLUENTIAL LEADERS

"Adrian Moldovan has an amazing story. He is one who has come through great tribulations. The wealth of powerful principles, scriptures and prayers Adrian shares in this book, will equip you for battle."

BISHOP NEIL C. ELLIS
2nd Presiding Bishop, Full Gospel Baptist Church Fellowship International
Senior Pastor, Mount Tabor Full Gospel Baptist Church, Nassau, Bahamas

"This book by Adrian Moldovan, is a book every believer in God should read. To me, it reads like something Thomas Paine or another one of our Founding Fathers would have written. So much of Adrian's book, testimony and experience are Bible inspired and fostered by the Writer of that Book..the Holy Spirit of God. The Bible urges "Let the redeemed of the Lord say so!" And again, "The salvation you seek is nigh thee, even in thy mouth!" And Jesus said to His disciples, paraphrasing, "Whatever you ask, using My name, you will receive, if you believe." We as a people have become too timid, too intimidated by our peers and our culture, to speak the truth. As children of the Most High God, we can "have what we say"...so it's time for us to say what we believe and demand that of our schools, our society and our government! God bless Adrian, this book, and those who read it and especially those who act on it."

PAT BOONE
Singer, Actor, Author, TV & Radio Personality, Producer

"In an age of much diagnosis and little resolution, Tell Hell No, offers not only a diagnostic of society's ills, but biblical repair through ageless tools. If employed, the renewal of the mind, devotion to God's Word, Prayer and Spirit filled confession, prove to be potent enough instruments to transform both the individual and nation."

PASTOR WAYNE CHANEY JR.
Senior Pastor, Antioch Church, Long Beach, California

"My dear brother and friend Adrian Moldovan, is uniquely equipped, gifted and empowered by God Himself, to communicate divine truth and the gospel of the Kingdom of God, across generational, racial and gender lines. Adrian Moldovan is authentic and genuine. He is a man of character, integrity and great communication skills. In an age like this where everything around us is falling apart, we need a sure word from the Lord. God has raised up at this hour, a young giant in the faith...a prophet, teacher and evangelist to proclaim the good news of the gospel, that will lead us to freedom, deliverance, hope, peace and power."

PASTOR WILLIAM DWIGHT MCKISSIC
Senior Pastor, Cornerstone Baptist Church, Arlington, Texas

Adrian Moldovan is a passionate and refreshing voice, that empowers people with his Christ centered wisdom. My team and I have personally experienced, what the world will experience, after reading "Tell Hell No."

DR. CRISTIN M. WALLACE, DDS
Nashville's Top Dentist for Professional Athletes
Exclusive Dentist to the Tennessee Titans

"In his book, Tell Hell No, Adrian Moldovan has boldly set his mouth to the trumpet, to sound the alarm. It is a cry for all of God's people to take their position of authority and become agents of change. It serves as a powerful tool, offering solutions to bring forth the will of God in your life and the life of those whom you love. Written with a Kingdom mindset, Tell Hell No, crosses all age barriers, cultural barriers and denominational barriers. My friend Adrian, has blessed us with a real hands on book."

PATRICIA ASHLEY
Founder of, Patricia Ashley Ministries
Author, and Speaker

"This wonderful book will inspire you to set bigger goals, persist through adversity and achieve wonderful things with your life."

BRIAN TRACY
President, Brian Tracy International
Legendary Speaker, Author & Entrepreneur

"Adrian Moldovan has a message that you need to hear. He breaks down how to "Tell Hell No" and Tell your life "YES!"

JONATHAN SPRINKLES
Voted Speaker of the Year, TV Personality, www.Jsprinkles.com

"In the book, Tell Hell No, Adrian Moldovan expresses very eloquently his passion for the gospel of Jesus Christ. His appreciation for the elements on which our country was established, is founded in a family background that gives him a perspective most of us can only imagine. It is an easy read that grabs your interest and will support your faith. There is a great deal of wisdom in his message , and I can also personally testify that his life supports his writing."

JOSEPH A. GRIMAUD
Former President of Precision Tune
Founder, City Light Coalition, Inc.
CEO, Grimaud Enterprises, Inc.

TELL HELL NO!

3 STEPS TO TRANSFORMING
YOUR LIFE, FAMILY & NATION.

ADRIAN MOLDOVAN

TELL HELL NO!
THREE STEPS TO TRANSFORMING YOUR LIFE, FAMILY AND NATION.

Copyright © 2013 by Adrian Moldovan

This publication contains the opinions and ideas of its author. The strategies outlined in this book are not guaranteed or warranted to produce any particular results. No warranty is made with respect to the accuracy or completeness of the information contained herein, and both the author and publisher specifically disclaim any responsibility for any liability, loss, or risk, personal or otherwise, which is incurred as a consequence, directly or indirectly, of use and application of any of the contents of this book.

All rights reserved. No portion of this book may be reproduced or transmitted in any form or by any means, electronic or mechanical, including photocopying and recording, or by any information storage or retrieval system without written permission of the publisher and author.

For written permission of use or information about special discounts for bulk purchases, please contact: Tell Hell No Ministries, at 1-803-739-6611.

All scripture quotations, unless otherwise indicated, are taken from the NKJV - the New King James Version. Copyright © 1954, 1958, 1982 by Thomas Nelson, Inc. Used by permission. All rights reserved.
NIV – Scriptures taken from the Holy Bible, New International Version ®. Copyright © 1973, 1978, 1984 by International Bible Society. Used by permission of Zondervan Publishing House. All rights reserved.
TLB – Scripture quotations marked (TLB) are taken from The Living Bible, copyright © 1971. Used by permission of Tyndale House Publishers, Inc. Wheaton, IL 60189. All rights reserved.

Printed in the United States of America

Library of Congress Cataloging-In-Publication Data

Moldovan, Adrian Emil
    Tell Hell No: Three steps to transforming your life, family and nation. / by Adrian Moldovan
        ISBN: 978-0-615-76545-7

It is my distinct honor and privilege, to dedicate this book to my grandfather Ion Moldovan. He paid the ultimate price of martyrdom, for refusing to be a silent witness for our Lord and Savior Jesus Christ. His legacy has ushered me into my destiny and for that, I am eternally grateful.

Love you Grandpa, I'll see you in the morning!

I HAVE FOUGHT THE GOOD FIGHT,
I HAVE FINISHED THE RACE,
I HAVE KEPT THE FAITH.

2 TIMOTHY 4:7

TABLE OF CONTENTS

FOREWORD BY BISHOP NEIL C. ELLIS...1
INTRODUCTION..4

1. WAKE UP...17
   - The Gray Fog...17
     - a. White House..18
     - b. Your House..22
     - c. God's House..26
   - The Solution..27

2. PREP UP..31
   - a. Think Up: The Mind is a Terrible Thing to Waste......................32
   - b. Word Up: No Deposit, No Withdrawal..38
   - c. Pray Up: Weapon of Mass Destruction..43

3. SPEAK UP..51
   - a. Who Should Speak Up?..53
   - b. When to Speak Up?...60
   - c. When Not to Speak Up?..63
   - d. How to Speak Up?...69
   - e. Where to Speak Up?...71
   - f. Cost of Speaking Up..77

CONCLUSION: TELL HELL, "NO!" 77

APPENDIX 1: SCRIPTURES 85
    a. Spiritual Foundations 88
    b. Biblical Applications for Life 92

APPENDIX 2: PRAYERS 115
    a. Prayers for Various Situations 116
    b. Prayers of the Bible 121
    c. Famous Prayers 124

ENDNOTES 129

FOREWORD

BY BISHOP NEIL C. ELLIS

"And do this, knowing the time, that now it is high time to awake out of sleep; for our salvation is nearer than when we first believed." - Romans 13:11

It is without a doubt, we are living in perilous times. The time when as the Bible states, "Men are becoming lovers of themselves, rather than lovers of God." While we are asleep, the enemy is using his best weapons, in his attempt to destroy our families, communities, churches, and countries. He has come as John 10:10 says, "To steal, kill and destroy."

Since the enemy is fulfilling his mandate, "To steal, kill and destroy," we must understand that it is "High time to awake out of sleep; for now our salvation is nearer then when we first believed." Those of us who are called to proclaim the good news, must stand up and speak up. As Edmund Burke remarked, "All that is necessary for the triumph of evil is that good men do nothing." We cannot continue to sit idly by and allow the enemy, to use people and circumstance to destroy our very foundations.

Adrian Moldovan has an amazing story. He is one who has come through great tribulations. He has experienced deportation, rejection, persecution, despair, low self-esteem and feeling like an absolute failure. But the hand of God was with him in the midst of the troubles he faced. Today, he is a passionate preacher of the gospel of Jesus Christ.

I commend Adrian for bringing to light, the fact that the Christian church must take a stand and maintain that stand. We must reclaim our families, communities, churches and nation for God. The message in this book will challenge you to rise up as a soldier in God's army. The book states firstly, we must wake up because while God will fight for us, He will do it through us. Secondly, we must prepare ourselves. The most powerful method of preparation is still prayer. Thirdly, we must know when and how to speak up.

According to Jesus, the test of the church's power is whether or not hell backs up when the church shows up. Jesus is on the offensive in building His Church and accomplishing His Agenda. He is not trying to stop the forces of hell and Satan, hell is trying to stop Him. The forces of hell are chasing the church. This means when it comes to the church and the forces against the church, the church is out front; no matter how it looks. So the test of our power, both individually and corporately as the body of Christ, is whether or not hell backs up when we show up. We've got to stop being on the defensive. The church is out front...we are not losing.

FOREWORD

The wealth of powerful principles, scriptures and prayers Adrian shares in this book, will equip you for battle. As you are faced with various challenges, always bear in mind, it is God's desire and will for you to walk in absolute victory. I am certain your life will be enriched, by following the principles laid out in this book. It is my desire, you would determine the need to show up, stand up, speak up; and when you speak up, as the title of this book indicates, you should "Tell Hell, No!"

BISHOP NEIL C. ELLIS CMG, DD, JP
2nd Presiding Bishop, Full Gospel Baptist Church Fellowship International
Chairman, Full Gospel Baptist Church Fellowship Bahamas
Senior Pastor, Mount Tabor Full Gospel Baptist Church, Nassau, Bahamas

INTRODUCTION

Today I am often characterized by others as being a confident, passionate, and uncompromising preacher of the Word of God. I readily admit these characteristics were not always present in my life. I was born in Romania when it was ruled by the communist dictator, Nicolae Ceausescu. Religious freedom as we know it today in America was nonexistent. There was no freedom of either religion or speech. Christians lived every single day with the impending threat of being beaten, tortured, incarcerated or martyred for the crime of simply voicing their faith. Living in this kind of hostile environment was nothing new for my family.

In 1919, my great-grandfather, Gheorghe Moldovan was publicly beaten for his faith until he lost consciousness. Officers were then ordered to drown him in the Danube River, but he escaped martyrdom when an overwhelming fear of God came upon the officers escorting him to the place where he was to be executed. They subsequently spared his life, ordering him to run away while they discharged their weapons into the air.

My grandfather Ion Moldovan, a Baptist pastor and evangelist, was often warned of the severe consequences he would incur if he continued to preach the

INTRODUCTION

gospel of Jesus Christ. He was interrogated, tortured and incarcerated many times for not compromising his faith. One Sunday evening after finishing his responsibilities at the church, he was run down by a truck and killed in a death arranged by the secret police. My grandfather paid the ultimate price of martyrdom, for refusing to be a silent witness for his Lord and Savior.

Following in the footsteps of my grandfather and great-grandfather, my father, Ioan Moldovan also endured severe persecution. In 1980, he was arrested, interrogated, beaten and sentenced, without a trial, to 25 years in prison for his unwavering evangelistic work, which the authorities called treason. After over 8,000 letters from Christians around the world were sent on his behalf, pleading for his freedom and protesting his imprisonment, the Romanian government decided it would be more politically beneficial for them to strip him and the rest of our family of our Romanian citizenship and expel us from our country and homeland.

> My grandfather paid the ultimate price of martyrdom for refusing to be a silent witness for his Lord and Savior.

In the fall of 1980, prior to deporting us from the country, the Romanian authorities confiscated all of my family's personal property including our home in Timisoara, which my father and grandfather built by hand. After saying painful goodbyes to our loved ones, our family of five boarded a plane in Romania bound for Rome. After being accepted as refugees in the United States, ten days later we landed in New York City with almost no knowledge of the English language, two suitcases and less than twenty dollars to our name. The sight of tears running down my mother's face, as she gazed through the airplane window at the Statue of Liberty and New York skyline, remains imprinted on my memory to this day. As a child I did not fully grasp all of the thoughts and emotions behind her tears, but looking back now, I understand them better. Freedom had come with a great price tag. We lost our Romanian citizenship, the physical presence of our friends and loved ones, our home, our personal belongings and the careers for which my father and mother spent years in study. Corrie ten Boom once said, "You may never know that Jesus is all you need, until Jesus is all you have." We lost everything, but Jesus.

> You may never know that Jesus is all you need, until Jesus is all you have.
> **- CORRIE TEN BOOM**

    Adjusting to the American culture proved to be painful for me. Although I was tremendously grateful to the Lord that by His grace, my family no longer endured being threatened and persecuted for our faith; I soon realized a consequence of our persecution was me being forced to adapt to a completely different environment. Not being able to speak a single word of English, made it even worse. This language barrier held me back in school for two years, resulting in me being branded as a "big dummy" throughout my early years of education. Compared to my parents and two sisters, I definitely was not the sharpest tool in the shed. When I would bring my report card home, the only positive comment my parents

INTRODUCTION

could make was, "At least we know he's not cheating." To compound the matter further, I had a speech impediment to overcome, as well. After preaching in Fort Worth, Texas, a few months ago, my sister, Gabriela and I spent an evening laughing about how God truly had a sense of humor in calling me to preach; we could still remember the times when I would shake like a leaf speaking in front of an audience unable to pronounce many of the English words I was trying to speak. Public speaking was not the career she or anybody else would have chosen for me!

Amongst, the many struggles and obstacles I had to overcome in my life, the two biggest ones were fear and rejection. No matter which way I turned, it seemed everyone required me to reach a standard, seemingly unattainable for me, just to be accepted by them. Society consistently demands you meet certain criteria before embracing you, as one of its own. When we came to this country and throughout my teenage life, my family was broke, busted and disgusted. In other words, we were poor. We were so poor we couldn't even "pay" attention!

Unfortunately, my peers demanded I look and dress a certain way to gain their approval and acceptance. This was not only true at the schoolhouse, but at the church house, as well. Physically, well, let's say, I was never considered a rival to Brad Pitt or Denzel Washington. Most of my life I struggled with being somewhat overweight. Even now people tell me they want to see a preacher at large, not a large preacher. Though my parents worked as hard as they could to provide for our needs, keeping up with the latest fashion craze was not a luxury we could afford. Most of the clothes we wore growing up were donated to us by the local church or bought from the local thrift store. Looking back at old pictures of myself, I now understand why I was made fun of, laughed at and frequently beaten up at school. The collars on some of the checkerboard patterned shirts I wore were so big you could jump off of the empire state building without a parachute and still land safely. Furthermore, it was tremendously difficult to meet the standard set for me at home. My parents, raised all of their life in the Romanian culture, found it difficult to understand and embrace various aspects of the American culture.

During the middle of my sophomore year in high school, although I had accepted Jesus into my heart, I found myself in my bedroom closet with a gun in my hand, fully convinced suicide was the only way out of the pain and anger I had built up over the years. For most of my young adult life I tried to gain value, self-worth and approval through meeting man's performance-based acceptance philosophy and I felt like I had failed miserably. Running through my mind over and over again were the painful words of rejection from those by whom I longed for their approval and acceptance. After hearing so many times that I was a stupid nobody and a loser who would never amount to anything, I was at the place where those lies had become my truth. Whoever came up with the statement "Sticks and stones may break my bones, but words will never hurt me," definitely lived in denial. That evening, in that dark closet, I felt the power of the Holy Spirit come upon me and comfort me in a way I had never felt before.

INTRODUCTION

Over the next three years God took me through the painful and difficult task of renewing my mind through His Word. Rather than accepting satan's lies that I was a loser, unworthy of love or acceptance, I made a commitment to embrace and believe only what God thought and said about me. When I felt as though my outward appearance didn't meet society's standard, I would quote Psalm 139:14, "I am wonderful and fearfully made." When I felt as if there was no purpose for my life, I quoted Jeremiah 29:11, "For I know the thoughts that I think toward you, says the Lord, thoughts of peace and not of evil, to give you a future and a hope." When I didn't think I could accomplish or succeed at a certain task because of my personal limitations, I would quote Philippians 4:13 "I can do all things through Christ who strengthens me." This was the first time in my life I truly understood what the Bible meant when it says that the power of life and death is in the tongue (Proverbs 18:21). One of the greatest lessons I learned while going through my deliverance process was that it was not what others said about me that caused the most spiritual, emotional and psychological damage, but what I was saying about myself. For years I thought my self-esteem and healing could only come through the validating voice of another human being, only to eventually realize God wanted to heal me from the inside out, rather than the outside in. I had to exchange man's external lie, for God's internal truth. When I changed what

> When I changed what I was confessing, I started to notice a difference in what I was possessing.

I was confessing, I started to notice a difference in what I was possessing. The Bible declares in Proverbs 6:2 that we are snared by the words of our mouth, not the words of others.

After graduating from high school, I wrestled with whether I should further my education in business or ministry. Ministry did not seem to offer a promising future, in light of my family history. Exile, persecution and martyrdom were all part of the benefits package I did not want to sign up for. Furthermore, the bible college where I ended up required two semesters of Greek and Hebrew. I had not mastered the English language and now they wanted me to learn Greek and Hebrew! Besides all that, who would want to listen to somebody who did not even have proper communication skills in the English language, much less Greek and Hebrew? Like Jonah, I tried to run from the assignment God had for my life, but He would not let me off of the hook that easily. One day while pondering on how far the grace of God had brought me, I realized everything I had been through in my life was nothing but a set up. God was preparing to birth a ministry out of my misery. It wasn't really about me... rather, it was about what God was preparing to do through me. Overcoming life's personal challenges through the power of the Holy Spirit is a wonderful thing! However, to be truly successful, spiritually, we need to produce successors for the Kingdom of God. For the first time in my life, I truly understood the tremendous value and responsibility of the anointing passed down to me through my father, grandfather and great-grandfather. Their spiritual history became my destiny. Today, I carry the mantle of being the fourth-generation preacher in my family. By the grace of God, I have been able to accomplish unfathomable things in my life. It would be foolish to think that I am where I am today because of my own initiative and strength. God, through my wife Holly, family members and close friends has consistently provided a voice to speak His truth into my life, no matter what obstacle I was facing. Without a doubt, my intelligent, beautiful, God-fearing wife is one of the greatest gifts God has ever blessed me with. God not only loves me through her, but uses her voice to guide me through my God-give purpose and destiny. The once fearful and timid Adrian Moldovan who considered himself to have no value or purpose in life, no longer operates according to that demonic, oppressed mindset. Today, I operate in the power of a different spirit, the Holy Spirit. 2 Timothy 1:7 declares, "For God has not given us a spirit of fear, but of power and of love and of a sound mind." I am who God says I am, I can do what God says I can do, and I can have what God says I can have. As a teacher, preacher, and evangelist, I am committed to winning the unsaved for Christ; encouraging and empowering the saved to live their lives to their fullest spiritual capacity.

> I have martyr's blood running through my veins and I refuse to be a silent witness for my Lord and Savior.

The passion, boldness, and confidence, through which I minister today, is a direct result of my personal relationship with my heavenly Father, Jesus Christ, and the godly legacy and anointing passed down to me through my family. I have martyr's blood running through my veins and I refuse to be a silent witness for my Lord and Savior. Today there are millions upon millions of people searching for the same thing I was once looking for... love, hope, acceptance and purpose. I believe, if God can transform the life of a rejected, fearful, timid individual, such as myself, He can transform your life, as well. My allegiance is to the inerrant and infallible Word of God and to my Lord and Savior, Jesus Christ. He died for me; I chose to live for Him.

> I am always amazed to see how God uses common, ordinary people to bring forth extraordinary change.

As I examine the state in which our nation currently finds itself, it is without a question, that our moral and spiritual compass is in dire need of a spiritual recalibration. The downward spiral in which our nation is continuing to head morally, educationally and financially is setting us on a course straight towards destruction. I've often wondered, what would have to happen for God's people to wake up and exercise their God-given right to speak up and use their voice to bring forth a spiritual transformation. I pray, we as a nation, do not have to hit rock bottom to be reminded that God is the rock at the bottom. He is the only sure foundation upon which we can build our future; as the old hymn, "The Solid Rock" declares, all other ground is sinking sand.

One of the things, I enjoy most is studying African-American history. If I could name one African-American individual whom I admire the most, it would have to be the woman most people call the initiator of the civil rights movement, Rosa Parks. I am always amazed to see how God uses common, ordinary people to bring forth extraordinary change, not only in their personal lives, but also in the lives of others. One day while reading the autobiography of Rosa Parks, "My Story," I came to the section where she describes what she was really thinking that cold December day in 1955, when she decided to take a stand against racial discrimination and segregation. She stated:

> No, the only tired I was, was tired of giving in.
> - **ROSA PARKS**

> "People always say that I didn't give up my seat because I was tired, but that isn't true. I was not tired physically, or no more tired than I usually was at the end of a working day. I was not old, although some people have an image of me as being old then. I was forty-two. No, the only tired I was, was tired of giving in."

True change in our personal life, family life and in the life of our nation, can only come to fruition when God's people get tired of giving in. When we finally get tired of giving in spiritually, physically, financially, emotionally, and relationally to the enemy, then and only then, will we see God's transforming power intervene in our lives.

The intent for writing this book, is not to criticize, condemn, or conjure up past mistakes of those of us who have missed opportunities to speak up or who have spoken up improperly in the past. Rather, my desire is that the material presented in this book will challenge and inspire you to once again attempt great things for God through the power of your spoken word. I certainly do not consider myself an expert on topic, but a student. I must confess; I have had my share of personal successes and failures, but like Paul, I do not count myself to have apprehended it yet, but I press towards the mark of the high calling of Jesus Christ. My desire is for you to fully use your voice, a God-given right, to bring forth the will of God into your personal life, your family's life, your community and the life of our nation. Regardless of the problems or challenges we may face today, God tells us in 2 Chronicles 7:14, "If My people who are called by My Name will humble themselves, and pray and seek My face, and turn from their wicked ways, then I will hear from heaven, and will forgive their sin and heal their land." He aslo states in Proverbs 18:21, "Death and life are in the power of the toungue..." As Christians, we have access to the King of Kings and Lord of Lords, the Creator of heaven and earth, whose eternal truth abides forever. God is calling His people to lift up their voices and Tell Hell, No! Your voice may be the spark that starts a fire all of hell cannot extinguish.

> God is calling His people to lift up their voices and Tell Hell, No!

THE
POWER
IS IN
YOUR
VOICE

CHAPTER 1

WAKE UP

THE GRAY FOG

We live in one of the most perplexing and dynamic times in the history of the United States of America. At one point in our nation's past we had a collective awareness of God. Now, however, our understanding of moral principles has become blurred. As a nation, we have pledged our allegiance to the kingdoms of this world, rather than the Kingdom of God, trusting politicians to offer us solutions to the problems that plague us. Any attempt to honestly discuss political and social issues is often met with animosity from all sides, leading to stalemates in Congress and state legislatures. Democrats, Republicans, conservatives, liberals, moderates, and everyone in between, disagree about fundamental principles previously shared by leaders of all political persuasions. In addition, we have put our hope in the power of the almighty dollar, yet the dollar itself, preaches to us whenever we look at it, by saying, "In God we trust." In so doing, it admonishes us to trust in God, rather than in it. Our confidence in money has been shaken, as a result of the sudden economic downturn, which has led many to question the financial infrastructure of our government. It seems no one can offer us a comprehensive solution. Compounding the issue is the fact that we are unwilling to take responsibility for our actions that led to the problem. We are like the proverbial father and son in therapy—the son entered the room and told the therapist, "I'm a loser because my dad is an alcoholic." The father, in his turn, had a very different perspective: "I'm an alcoholic," he explained, "because my son is a loser." In the same manner, we also struggle to take responsibility for the problems in our society, choosing instead, to ignore them or demand the government fix them. We are facing big problems from the White House, to the courthouse, to the schoolhouse, to our own houses, and no easy solution presents itself. We are living in a gray fog of uncertainty during these increasingly volatile times.

WHITE HOUSE

In recent years it has become apparent our country is in a societal and political tailspin. We have gradually strayed from our nation's foundational Christian principles and are heading deep into a pluralistic, "anything goes" culture. We are actively moving away from the moral foundation upon which our political system was built, by attempting to divorce our policies from the very logic that formed them. Recently it seems the political sector is becoming increasingly and actively antagonistic toward Christianity.

For example, America, like any functional government, has a court system to carry out justice. Legal infractions result in punishment to maintain a well-ordered society. We enforce laws regarding robbery, murder, false testimony and juvenile delinquency. Laws like these were handed down to Moses by God, in the form of the Ten Commandments (Exodus 20:12, 14-16). This is part of our legal heritage, founded on morality as defined in Exodus through the Ten Commandments. We received these commandments from God, yet some courthouses were required to remove displays of the Ten Commandments from their premises, on the basis such displays, show favoritism toward Judeo-Christian religion.[1] Perhaps someone should sue the legal system for plagiarism, because God is the author of those commandments and He's not getting any credit! Those laws did not originate in the mind of any Senator or Supreme Court justice. The Bible states that these laws are written on our hearts by God (Romans 2:15). This is just one small example of the many ways in which our nation is abandoning its firm foundation of Christian morality.

Something very similar is happening with regard to prayer in the public arena. Oddly enough, though our children are no longer allowed to pray in public schools, last year the chaplain of the House and the chaplain of the Senate were paid a combined total of $311,699.84 by taxpayers, to open their respective meetings in prayer.[2,3] How is it they get paid such a large amount of money for praying in public, but our children are not allowed to pray publicly in school for free?

Last year, the United States spent over $8,600,000 on environmental concerns.[4] The Bay checkerspot butterfly, the valley elderberry longhorn beetle, the tiger salamander, and the Alameda whipsnake, are just a few of the insects and animals that benefitted from this money.[5] The Bible is very clear that environmental preservation is important and valuable. Genesis states: "And God blessed them, and God said unto them, be fruitful, and multiply, and fill the earth, and subdue it: and have dominion over the fish of the sea, and over the fowl of the air, and over every living thing that moves upon the earth," (Genesis 1:28). God gave us the earth and we certainly ought to take care of it the best we can.

> We are placing a higher value on animal life, than we do on human life, created in God's own image.

However, our national budget indicates we have misplaced our priorities. In that same year we spent over eight million dollars to save the lives of insects and animals, over one million abortions were performed.[6] We are placing a higher value on animal life, than we do on human life, created in God's own image. "So God created man in his own image, in the image of God created He him; male and female created He them," (Genesis 1:27). The fact that humanity is created in God's image is what separates man from animals and grants every human being an inestimable value. Unfortunately, our value system has been turned upside down. We have more allegiance to an insect or an animal than to our own children, created in God's image!

In addition, in 2012 our president, Barack Obama publically and proudly endorsed "gay" marriage and called for its legalization.[7] Many people may think, *"What's the big deal?* It's not like he's mandating that you embrace it. People should be able to do what they want!" Yes, America is a country where freedom of speech is strongly valued. However, the President's endorsement has and will continue to negatively affect society at large. The President of the United States wields a great deal of power and influence. Now that the executive branch of government has officially endorsed the practice of same-sex marriage, it is only a matter of time before such endorsements trickle down to the living rooms of the nation. The federal government has already passed hate crime legislation that could hold pastors accountable for saying anything against homosexuality. This type of radical shift in family values will affect every generation that follows. Nationally and politically, we do not recognize the importance of the biblical family unit, like we once did. This failure will have lasting repercussions. Our president needs to remember we are all residence of a world we did not create. Until we have the power to create our own world, it would be wise to comply with the moral laws God established to govern His world.

Needless to say, we can clearly see our nation straying from biblical morality in many areas. Christianity is met with hostility in major political and social venues. In the book of Judges, the Bible speaks about a similar situation in Israel. "Every man did that which was right in his own eyes," (Judges 21:25). In the same way, Americans are now doing what is right in their own

> God has blessed America, has America blessed God?

eyes, and an objective notion of right and wrong has all but disappeared. America claims it wants God to bless America, but America does not want to be a nation under Him. A bumper sticker said it well when it proclaimed, "God has Blessed America, has America Blessed God?"

YOUR HOUSE

The aforementioned political issues are closely linked to a profound shift in cultural values. As issues such as abortion, divorce and same-sex marriage have attained increasingly widespread acceptance, our understanding of human values and the importance of the family has naturally been affected.

God created marriage and the family for a variety of reasons. First, marriage is meant to be a reflection of God's covenant relationship with His people. Paul makes it clear in Ephesians 5:22-32, the unwavering and sacrificial union between a married couple was intended to demonstrate Christ's selfless love and unconditional sacrifice for the world. Secondly, God created the family as a means of protecting and instilling values in children (Ephesians 6:4; Proverbs 22:6). Finally, stable family units form the basis of a stable society. In all these ways, it is apparent that following God's rules for morality is both commanded and beneficial to us. Unfortunately, our culture today is in open rebellion against God's commandments and His perfect will for us.

The statistics are sobering. Teen births, while gradually declining, still peak at around 400,000 a year, with the result that we have many girls who are barely out of childhood themselves trying to raise children.[8] Additionally, 1 out of 4 women will be a victim of domestic violence during their lifetime.[9] The FBI estimates there are over 1.4 million active gang members in the United States which often times serve as substitute families .[10] All of these statistics are reminders of how imperative it is to bring God back into our homes.

> 1 out of 4 women will be a victim of domestic violence during their lifetime.

Today there are many barriers that serve to keep parents from fulfilling their Godly duties to train up their children in the way they should go. Due to the current economic downturn, there has been an increase in family homelessness and poverty. Many parents are forced to work two jobs just to make ends meet. According to current estimates, there are approximately 16.1 million children in the United States currently living in poverty. There are about 50.1 million Americans that are food insecure and constantly at risk of going hungry.[11]

One of the most glaring examples of shifting attitudes towards the family, is embodied in the fact that over 54 million abortions were performed in the United States, since the 1973 Supreme Court decision legalizing abortion on demand.[12] These lives lost, as a result of the Roe v. Wade decision, were endorsed by many of our citizens. This permissive attitude towards abortion in our nation is troubling. We allow our unborn babies to be killed in the womb as people claim it is their "right to choose," without considering that the child involved is never given a choice in the matter. Human life used to be valued as a miraculous gift; now, it has become a commodity that we feel free to toss aside like a used dishrag when it threatens to become a roadblock to our careers and personal dreams.

> The observed traits of the parents often become the practiced behaviors of the children.

Divorce is another issue drastically impacting the family unit. Every year since 1980, the divorce rate in the United States has been higher than the rates in Canada, Japan, Denmark, France, Germany, Ireland, Italy, the Netherlands, Spain, Sweden and the United Kingdom.[13] It seems as though our nation values the family unit far less than it ever has. This has led to a casual attitude toward the institution of marriage itself. We've begun to view marriage primarily as a means of personal fulfillment, rather than a sacred picture of Christ and the Church. Therefore, entering into and leaving marriages, based on little more than our ever-changing feelings and desires. With many Hollywood stars switching partners every few years, in the same manner they perform a wardrobe change, our society is constantly making a mockery of the sacred institution of marriage. Alec Baldwin, an actor currently starring in the hit show 30 Rock, summed up the matter-of-fact view of divorce in a recent interview, when he advised fans, "If you do get married, get a pre-nup....It's about having a document that states how you'll dissolve your marriage while you still have a shred of respect for each other."[14] This attitude is planning for failure before the vows are even exchanged.

Marriage is increasingly viewed as an obsolete institution, leaving the core of the family unit on shaky ground. This is especially troubling when one considers the impact of divorce on the children involved in the relationship. While there are certain situations where single parenthood is the only option; such as a deceased, unfaithful or abusive spouse, children facing these circumstances are in no way destined to a lifetime of failure. God provided strength, provision and a promise to Hagar, the first single mother mentioned in the Bible, that He would make her son a great nation. In the same way, God will make sure that a child being raised by a single parent will have the proper relationships, finances and grace to accomplish their God-given purpose and destiny.

However, in many instances, divorce begins a negative cycle in the family. The observed traits of the parents often become the practiced behaviors of the children. Our society's "anything goes" attitude towards marriage, is setting up future generations to have to deal with the painful ramifications and consequences of divorce. This will result in more children being hurt, who in the long run may not know how to properly value the sanctity of the biblical family. It's our choice, as to whether we pass along generational curses or blessings to our children. At the moment we seem to be choosing unwisely.

GOD'S HOUSE

Since we have not been able to find solutions in the White House or our own houses, our hope is that we could find them in God's house, the Church. Unfortunately to a large degree, this is not so.

Martin Luther King, Jr. once candidly stated, "It is appalling that the most segregated hour of Christian America is eleven o'clock on Sunday morning."[15] Despite the fact that this speech was given in 1963, its words are applicable more than ever; in 2013; and we are not limited to racial divisions. Social, cultural, political and denominational differences constantly keep us separated. The unity Jesus prayed for in John 17:23, "I in them, and You in Me; that they may be made perfect in one, and that the world may know that You have sent Me, and have loved them as You have loved Me," is rarely to be found collectively in the Body of Christ.

> The Christian silent majority, has become the number one tool in the hand of the enemy, contributing to the spiritual decline of America.

Furthermore, we have begun to embrace a vague "spirituality" rooted in a humanistic, rather than a biblical worldview. Rather than valuing God's truth, we base our actions, thoughts and convictions on whatever our feelings dictate at the moment. We have fallen in love with the values of Hollywood rather than the Holy Word of God. But our feelings should never usurp biblical truth. Truth, as set forth in God's Word, is unchanging regardless of our culture and personal feelings.

Unfortunately, many churches are not utilizing the truth they have to bring about true long lasting change in the culture around them. Instead, they are choosing to stay silent in the face of a sweeping cultural change. The Christian silent majority, has become the number one tool in the hand of the enemy, contributing to the spiritual decline of America. While one of the original purposes of the Church was that "through the church the manifold wisdom of God might now be made known to the rulers and authorities in the heavenly places." We have lost our edge. George Whitefield, the great evangelist once proclaimed, "The Christian world is in a deep sleep, nothing but a loud shout can awaken them out of it." The Church has to awaken from its sleep. It is one thing for us to be rejected, but as the body of Christ, we can no longer afford to be ignored.

THE SOLUTION

We have seen how the enemy is in the process of destroying our nation, our churches and tearing apart our families. He has come like the thief in John 10:10, to "...kill, steal, and destroy." God's people have to step up to the plate and meet the challenges at hand. We need to do more than just have church; we need to be the Church. Christians often have the erroneous mindset that if we would only pray hard enough, then we can sit back with a bucket of popcorn and watch God fight our battles for us. This is partly true. We absolutely should pray. However, what we need to realize is that God doesn't want to fight our battles for us; he wants to fight our battles through us. We must accept that we are part of the solution to the problems, we have been praying for. If our Goliaths are going to be defeated, we must find our slingshots and our five smooth stones. If we are going to see countless people emancipated from being enslaved by the enemy, like Moses, we must pick up our rod. If the Jericho walls that hold our God-given inheritance are going to fall, we must walk around them seven times. We cannot just sit idly by and wait for heaven to fight our earthly battles. God is not looking for an audience; He is looking for an army who is willing to fight the good fight of faith.

> God is not looking for an audience; He is looking for an army who is willing to fight the good fight of faith.

Practically, though, how can we fight? How can we best address our culture in its steady decline from its biblical values and bring forth personal and corporate change? The power to fight is not in our fists; nor is it solely in the political arena. The power to fight is not even primarily in our wallets. The power to fight is in our mouths. As Christians, our voice is our main weapon to create a God-honoring environment for our nation and our families, and to defeat the enemy in every area of our lives. Genesis 1:2 states that when God saw that the earth was chaotic, formless and void, He used the creative power of His spoken word to bring forth structure, order and change. The phrase "God said" is mentioned ten times in the creation account of Genesis, letting us know that whenever God speaks, something always happens and whatever God speaks will always come to past. Since God created us in His image, He has deposited in our spiritual DNA the same creative ability to build up His kingdom and bring forth change through the power of the spoken word. The power to bring forth change is in your words. In Mark 11:23, Jesus said "Whosoever shall say unto this mountain, Be thou removed, and be thou cast into the sea; and shall not doubt in his heart, but shall believe that those things which he saith shall come to pass; he shall have whatsoever he saith." He also promises us that He will supply whatever we ask in His name (John 14:13-14). We can only reclaim our nation, our churches and our families, when we choose to raise our God-given voices, to tell Hell, "No" and bring forth change and transformation, through the power of the spoken word.

THE POWER IS IN YOUR VOICE

CHAPTER 2
PREP UP

"By failing to prepare, you are preparing to fail."
Benjamin Franklin

Every individual who has joined the Army knows, that no matter how passionate they are about fighting for their country, they must first endure the demanding task of graduating from boot camp. Heading into battle without proper training is a guaranteed recipe for disaster. Unfortunately, in the same way, many Christians today are excited to enlist in the Army of the Lord, yet tragically find themselves frustrated and spiritually defeated when failing to properly prepare for spiritual warfare. Telling Hell, "No!" is a bold and noble deed, but if we speak up without prepping up, we will get beat up by the enemy.

    Our minds, our knowledge of the Word of God and our prayer lives are key elements of our Christian walk. They must be developed before entering into effective spiritual warfare. To advance the Kingdom of God, we must have the mind of Christ, we must know the Word of God and we must always begin our spiritual battles on our knees in prayer. This chapter deals with the "prep" work necessary, in these three areas, for every believer who hopes to emerge from a spiritual battle victorious.

THINK UP:
THE MIND IS A TERRIBLE THING TO WASTE

"For though we walk in the flesh, we do not war according to the flesh. For the weapons of our warfare are not carnal but mighty in God for pulling down strongholds, casting down arguments and every high thing that exalts itself against the knowledge of God, bringing every thought into captivity to the obedience of Christ."
-2 Corinthians 10:3-5

Whether or not we acknowledge it, you and I are in a spiritual battle every minute and hour of every day. This battle between the Kingdom of God and the kingdom of darkness cannot be escaped or ignored. 1 Peter 5:8 warns us that the devil is always prowling about like a roaring lion, looking for someone to devour. As believers and soldiers in the army of the Lord we do not have the option to play the proverbial ostrich with its head in the sand, hoping our enemy will somehow overlook or ignore us. We have two choices: stand up and fight the good fight of faith or, as John 10:10 states, continue to allow the enemy to steal, kill and destroy everything that is rightfully ours through Christ Jesus our Lord.

To defeat the enemy, we must first understand the mind is the battlefield upon which all spiritual warfare begins. Our adversary knows whoever controls your mind will ultimately have control of you, your family, your church, and your community. 2 Corinthians 10:3-4 clearly states that we cannot fight spiritual battles through our own fleshly tactics. Human methodologies and ideologies may produce temporary results, but they will not achieve long term victory. This is why a prideful self-help philosophy will always eventually lead to spiritual defeat. A person may have more degrees than a thermometer and think they have reached the apex of intellectualism, yet still be defeated by the enemy. This is why Paul writes, "Let this mind be in you which was also in Christ Jesus" (Philippians 2:5).

> We cannot change our hearts, but we can change our minds; and when we change our minds, God will change our hearts.
> **- VANCE HAVNER**

Taking control of our thoughts is critical because they directly impact our actions. Every action a person commits is preceded by a corresponding thought. Before I *steal* the cookie, I *think* about opening the cookie jar. If you want to know the direction in which someone is headed, all you have to do is observe their pattern of thinking. The person who is thinking of food will soon be headed towards the kitchen. The person who is constantly dwelling on God's Word will probably be headed to the nearest Bible. Our thoughts will always beat us to the destination toward which we are travelling.

Proverbs 23:7 states "For as a man thinks in his heart, so he is," equating our entire being with the thoughts pondered in our heart. Thoughts are not merely entities that exist in our head, but in effect they are the barometer by which we can measure the depth of our soul. Our actions can be predicted by our thoughts and our character can be judged by them.

> Your beliefs become your thoughts, Your thoughts become your words, Your words become your actions, Your actions become your habits, Your habits become your values, Your values become your destiny.
> - **MAHATMA GANDHI**

Our thought patterns tend to be shaped by three sources: our experiences, satan and God, through the Holy Spirit. First, our senses and personal experiences, both past and present, contribute tremendously to our thought processes. These experiences are comprised of events that took place throughout our lives, leading all the way back to childhood. For example, if you were raised in a performance based acceptance home where you always had to "do the right thing" to receive love and acceptance, you might be prone to develop a mindset of self-condemnation and have difficulty believing God's unconditional love applies to you. If, on the other hand, you were raised in an environment where you were loved unconditionally, you are more likely to understand and accept God's love and sacrifice for you, as the ultimate declaration of your value and acceptance.

While our experiences can influence our thoughts,

they will only control us if we choose to give them that power. As believers, we should always run our experience-based thoughts through the grid of Scripture before we embrace them. This protects us from allowing satan to twist our experiences into ungodly beliefs, which can produce any number of spiritual maladies, such as pride or insecurity. The aforementioned person who grew up in a home, wherein they had to perform to be accepted, might look to Scripture and find God loved and valued us enough to send His Son Jesus to die for us while we were still sinners (Romans 5:8). This biblical truth gives the individual an understanding of their true value in Christ, which enables them to reject thoughts about needing to perform, to gain love and acceptance. Even if they wrestle with negative thoughts for a period of time, they can overcome them by choosing to replace them with the truth of God's Word.

    In addition to our experiences, satan can be another source from which our thoughts are derived. When I initially became a believer, I expected that as a result of walking down the aisle and praying the Sinner's Prayer, I would no longer struggle with sin. I assumed that 2 Corinthians 5:17, which says "...old things have passed away; behold, all things have become new" meant I would become instantly holy and my sinful patterns would painlessly disappear. Instead, I found myself struggling with the same ungodly thoughts and temptations which I wrestled with prior to my conversion. What I had failed to realize was, my conversion was foremost a spiritual one. Jesus tells his followers that "...unless one is born of water and the Spirit, he cannot enter the kingdom of God.

That which is born of the flesh is flesh, and that which is born of the Spirit is spirit. Do not marvel that I said to you, 'You must be born again.'" (John 3:5-7).

When we receive Jesus Christ as our personal Lord and Savior, we experience a rebirth of our human spirit. This does not, however, result into instant perfection, as Romans 12:2 makes clear: "And do not be conformed to this world, but be transformed by the renewing of your mind, that you may prove what is good and acceptable and perfect will of God." What the Apostle Paul is conveying in this text, is although our soul is saved upon conversion, our mind is still in the process of being renewed. Every day satan is doing everything he can to control your mind. God on the other hand wants to transform your mind through the power of the Holy Spirit and His Word.

The Holy Spirit is the only One who can prevent satan or our past experiences from dictating our thought life. When a person's spirit is saved through the power of the Holy Spirit, that individual no longer needs to rely

> There are many locks in my house and all with different keys, but I have one master-key which opens them all. The Lord has many treasures and secrets all shut up from carnal minds with locks which they cannot open. But he who walks in fellowship with Jesus possesses the master-key which will open to him all the blessings of the covenant and even the very heart of God
>
> **- CHARLES SPURGEON**

on their senses or experiences to control their thoughts. As Romans 8:5-6 states, "Those who live according to the flesh have their minds set on what the flesh desires; but those who live in accordance with the Spirit have their minds set on what the Spirit desires. The mind governed by the flesh is death, but the mind governed by the Spirit is life and peace." Furthermore, according to John 14:26, God has sent the Holy Spirit to teach us and remind us of God's truth. If you allow the Holy Spirit to rule over your mind, you will not only live a victorious Christian life, but you will have at your disposal, One who will constantly help you, teach you and remind you of God's truth. (Wow, that sounds like a great three for one special to me!)

At times, it can be hard to tell what promptings are of God and which are of the devil. For example, it is not uncommon for believers to live with a sense of condemnation for sins committed in the past. While this may feel like a proper response to sin, we know from Scripture, satan is the accuser of the brethren (Job 1:6; Revelation 12:10), and that "...there is now no condemnation for those who are in Christ Jesus" (Romans 8:1). Once we confess our sin to God, He removes it as far from us as "the east is from the west" (Psalm 103:12). On the other hand, we also know from Scripture that the Spirit guides us in righteousness, so there may be times when we feel conviction for a sin from which we haven't yet repented. Once again, we can gauge the legitimacy of our thoughts and feelings via the lens of Scripture, for the Word of God guides us in all truth and righteousness and helps us distinguish the voice of truth from that of lies. The rule of thumb for determining if the thoughts about your past sins are from God or satan is simply this; what does the conviction you are feeling prompt you to do? If it is prompting you to confess your sin, then the feeling is from the Holy Spirit. Thoughts of condemnation and hopelessness are from satan. He does not want you to experience liberty in Christ, but desires to keep you in spiritual bondage.

WORD UP:
NO DEPOSIT, NO WITHDRAWAL

"For the word of God is living and powerful, and sharper than any two-edged sword, piercing even to the division of soul and spirit, and of joints and marrow, and is a discerner of the thoughts and intents of the heart."
- Hebrews 4:12

If we are going to be a generation that will Tell Hell, "No!" and be willing to charge into the enemy's camp to advance the Kingdom of God, we must not only have a renewed Christ-like mindset, but we must utilize the "sword of the Spirit, which is the Word of God" (Ephesians 6:17). God has given us His Word as both the offensive and defensive weapon, ideally suited for spiritual warfare with the enemy.

Matthew 4:1-11 reveals one of the most important and monumental spiritual battles encountered by our General, Jesus Christ, while He was here on earth.

"Then Jesus was led up by the Spirit into the wil-

derness to be tempted by the devil. And when He had fasted forty days and forty nights, afterward He was hungry. Now when the tempter came to Him, he said, "If You are the Son of God, command that these stones become bread." But He answered and said, "It is written, 'Man shall not live by bread alone, but by every word that proceeds from the mouth of God.' Then the devil took Him up into the holy city, set Him on the pinnacle of the temple, and said to Him, "If You are the Son of God, throw Yourself down. For it is written: 'He shall give His angels charge over you,' and, 'In their hands they shall bear you up, lest you dash your foot against a stone.' Jesus said to him, "It is written again, 'You shall not tempt the Lord your God.' Again, the devil took Him up on an exceedingly high mountain, and showed Him all the kingdoms of the world and their glory. And he said to Him, "All these things I will give You if You will fall down and worship me." Then Jesus said to him, "Away with you, satan! For it is written, 'You shall worship the Lord your God, and Him only you shall serve.' Then the devil left Him, and behold, angels came and ministered to Him."

In this showdown between the Kingdom of God and the kingdom of darkness, Jesus clearly exemplifies the importance of knowing and using the Word of God to defeat the enemy. Each time He was tempted by satan, Jesus responded with, "It is written." He could have called ten thousand angels or used any number of other methods to triumph over the devil. Instead of respond-

> The deceit, the lie of the devil, consists of this: that he wishes to make man believe that he can live without God's word.
> - **DIETRICH BONHOEFFER**

ing to the devil with new words, He chose to use the written Word of God, from the book of Deuteronomy, to defeat the enemy. As 2 Timothy 3:16 says, "All Scripture is given by the inspiration of God, and is profitable for doctrine, for reproof, for correction, for instruction in righteousness." In other words, God's Word provides us with everything we need to walk the Christian walk.

It is interesting to note, even though Jesus was physically exhausted after fasting for forty days and nights, He never retreated or backed down from the confrontation. Christ relied on his spiritual inner strength to battle the enemy regardless of his physical condition. No matter how weak a believer feels, the Word of God provides the power to be a victor, not a victim, when the believer chooses to use it. Spiritual battles are fought from the inside out; that is, our victory depends not on us, but on the Spirit within us. This is why David wrote in Psalms 119:11, "Thy word have I hid in mine heart, that I might not sin against thee." If we really want to overcome the enemy in the spirit realm, we must practice wielding our spiritual sword, the Word... by hearing it, studying it, and memorizing it, on a daily basis.

If we want to maintain continual access to the power of God's Word, we must be intentionally seeking to become intimately acquainted with it. Marine Corps pilots regularly use the Naval Air Training and Operating

Procedures Standardization (NATOPS) manual. The purpose of this manual is to provide them with important answers to every situation they might face in the air. As such, it is unique to their particular aircraft. For instance, if you have a left engine fail and a right hydraulic pump fail, what do you do? Suppose your rudder sticks and the flaps will not lower to the full open position? They study the NATOPS manual because in the event of an emergency, they need to be able to recall what to do in an instant. Despite their having successfully completed pilot's school, they will be seen studying the manual for hours before a flight. They have enough wisdom to know, they can never be too familiar, with what is basically the "Bible" for their plane. The same should be true of us, with the eternal Word of God that never changes.

We can increase our familiarity with the Word in any number of ways. Sermons, Bible studies and personal devotions are some of the most common ways. Another simple way to increase your daily intake of the Word, is to find the Bible on audiotape and listen to it while driving. Christian music can also provide opportunities to hear God's Word, as can Christian books and sermons accessed online throughout the week.

> A Bible which is falling apart usually belongs to someone who isn't. The key to victory is "it is written."
> - **C H SPURGEON**

The most effective way to become familiar with God's Word is, of course, to study it. There are a number of resources pertaining to studying the Word of God available at your local Christian bookstore. Christian resources are great, but reading the actual scriptures yourself, rather than exclusively relying on what someone else says about them, is critical to a healthy devotional life. Commentaries are available online and at your local library to help you study scripture passages more deeply, but these are best consulted only after you have read and studied the passage on your own.

One of the most powerful and possibly least used methods of becoming familiar with the Word of God, is memorizing it. Memorizing can feel like tedious work up front, but the benefits you reap from having the Word of God at your fingertips, is well worth the investment. You may want to consider setting a scripture memorization goal (i.e.; a verse a week) and then leave index cards with those verses on it all over your house, in your car and in your purse or wallet. Then you can use any free time you might have while, standing in a line, waiting at a red light, or getting ready for the day, for memorizing scripture. Read and re-read the verses using the index cards as prompts, but slowly wean yourself off of them until you can say the entire verse from memory. In Appendix 1, located in the back of this book, are scriptures listed categorically to help you access the Word of God quickly whenever facing a particular challenge. They can serve as a tremendous resource for you, to enhance your scripture memory and prayer life. Building up your arsenal before entering into a spiritual battle is critical. Remember no deposit, no withdrawal. You must have the Word of God deposited on the inside, to confront the enemy on the outside.

PRAY UP:
WEAPON OF MASS DESTRUCTION

"...praying always with all prayer and supplication in the Spirit, being watchful to this end with all perseverance and supplication for all the saints." — Ephesians 6:18

Besides capturing our thoughts and becoming proficient in our knowledge of the Word of God, we must access yet another spiritual weapon, if we are to be effective warriors for Christ. Prayer is the Christian's "weapon of mass destruction." Regrettably, we Christians have a propensity to allow satan to trick us into adopting a lackadaisical or lethargic attitude towards him and his cohorts; a very dangerous mistake. After all, since the Bible says, God knows what we need before we even ask for it, some erroneously adopt the mindset that there is no need to pray.

1 Peter 5:8 states "Be sober, be vigilant; because your adversary the devil walks about like a roaring lion, seeking whom he may devour." In other words there is never a moment in time, when our enemy calls for a cease-fire or takes a break from his John 10:10 stealing, killing and destroying job duties; we can't afford to let our guard down. Elizabeth Elliot, Christian author and speaker, and widow of martyr Jim Elliot, does an excellent job illustrating the importance of prayer in her book, Love Has a Price Tag.

People who ski, I suppose, are people who happen to like skiing, who have time for skiing, who can afford to ski, and who are good at skiing. Recently I found that I often treat prayer as though it were a sport like skiing-something you do if you like it, something you do in your spare time, something you do if you can afford the trouble, something you do if you're good at it....

But prayer isn't a sport. It's work. Prayer is no game.... Prayer is the opposite of leisure. It's something to be engaged in, not indulged in. It's a job you give priority to. It's performing when you have energy left for nothing else. "Pray when you feel like praying," somebody has said. "Pray when you don't feel like praying. Pray until you do feel like praying." If we Pray only at our leisure—that is, at our own convenience—can we be true disciples? Jesus said "Anyone who wants to follow me must put aside his own desires and conveniences." (Luke 9:23, TLB).

In the wrestling of a Christian in prayer, "our fight is not against any physical enemy: it is against organizations and powers that are spiritual. We are up against the unseen power that controls this dark world, and spiritual agents from the very headquarters of evil" (Ephesians 6:112, Phillips). Seldom do we consider the nature of our opponent, and that is to his advantage. When we do recognize him for who he is, however, we have an inkling as to why prayer is never easy. It's the weapon that the unseen power dreads most, and if he can get us to treat it as casually as we treat a pair of skis or tennis racquet, he can keep his hold.[1]

Prayer is one of the Christian's most powerful weapons against the enemy. It provides a lifeline to connect us to our Commander-in-chief. No solider enters a battle without first receiving precise orders from their commander. No matter how much Scripture we have stockpiled in our spiritual warehouses, victory cannot be attained without prayer.

This is why Paul, under the leading of the Holy Spirit, commands every believer in Ephesians 6:18 to always pray. He further reiterates this in 1 Thessalonians 5:17 where he states that we ought to pray without ceasing. Jesus urged his disciples in Luke 18:1 to pray always and not lose heart, reminding them where the true source of their strength lies. Therefore, it is without question or debate; Scripture mandates every believer to engage in unceasing, vigilant and effective prayer.

> Victory cannot be attained without prayer.

During Desert Storm, prior to sending in the ground forces, the US military spent days, with an air assault on the enemy's positions. This carpet bombing was intended to "soften the enemy up," to make the work of the ground forces that much easier. When our ground forces crossed the border into Iraq, there was almost no resistance. This was because the aerial bombardment had destroyed one of the largest militaries in the world. In the same way, we need to carpet bomb the enemies terrain with prayer, before entering into hand-to-hand combat with our adversary.

If anyone would qualify to be exempted from having to pray, it would have been Jesus, the Son of God. Yet we see him praying at His baptism in Luke 3:21. We see Him praying part of the day and all night before He chose His twelve disciples in Luke 6:12. We see in Luke 5:16, Jesus withdrawing into the wilderness to pray to renew His strength after ministering and healing the crowds. He prays at Lazarus' tomb in John 11:41, before raising him from the dead. Near the end of his life on earth, He prayed in the Garden of Gethsemane in Luke 22:41, before enduring the suffering and shame of being crucified. Even while He was on the cross, Jesus never ceased to communicate with His Heavenly Father. Now if Jesus, the Son of God wrapped up in flesh, had to depend on prayer to accomplish His purpose here on earth, how much more should we.

One day after Jesus had finished praying, one of the disciples said "Lord teach us to pray." The disciples had seen Jesus feed five thousand men, plus women and children, with two fish and five loaves of bread. They were there when he gave sight to the blind man and raised Lazarus from the dead. Having seen these miracles, one might have thought they would have asked Jesus, to teach them how to heal the sick, raise the dead or cast out devils, but instead they asked Him to teach them how to pray. The disciples had often times seen Jesus retreat in isolation to pray. After observing this pattern in His life, they came to the conclusion that whatever He was doing in private, was causing Him to be so powerful in public.

Believers, often times, shy away from praying because they feel they are not adequately equipped to pray. Yet it is important to note, that Jesus did not chastise His disciples for asking Him to teach them how to pray. Jesus could have said "After being with me all of this time, you should know how to pray." No, He simply and lovingly began to instruct them. Satan, knowing the power of prayer, will try to make us feel unworthy of approaching God, when we lack proficiency in our prayer lives. However, we must remember prayer is not caught, but taught. The Bible says ask and it shall be given, knock and the door will be opened, seek and you shall find. Spiritual victory can only be achieved through a persistent commitment to prayer, for prayer is the believer's "weapon of mass destruction," to ensure victory for every spiritual battle.

> Everyday I pray. I yield myself to God, the tensions and anxieties go out of me and peace and power come in.
> **- DALE CARNEGIE**

Prayer can be difficult at first and it is not uncommon for individuals to become discouraged and give up following a few "failed" attempts to develop a consistent and habitual prayer life. Though it does not come naturally, rest assured praying will become easier with consistent practice. If you need help getting started, there are a variety of books on prayer available, but one of the best ways to learn how to pray is by consulting God's Word. Many of the Psalms can be read as prayers. Some of Paul's letters, such as Ephesians, Philippians, and Colossians, contain prayers that may serve as great examples. The Gospels, Matthew, Mark, Luke and John, provide wonderful illustrations of Christ praying, that may also be helpful in expanding your ability to pray. In the back of this book, Appendix 2 offers various examples of prayers. They provide a blue print to guide you as you develop your own method of praying. The Bible warns us in Matthew 6:7-8 to not merely recite memorized prayers, which can lead to vain repetition, but to pray in a manner that is transparent before God. A professor once said "All of us have one routine prayer in our system; and once we get rid of it, then we can really start to pray."

> All of us have one routine prayer in our system; and once we get rid of it, then we can really start to pray.
> - **AUTHOR UNKNOWN**

THE POWER IS IN YOUR VOICE

CHAPTER 3
SPEAK UP

"No weapon formed against you shall prosper, And every tongue which rises against you in judgment you shall condemn. This is the heritage of the servants of the Lord, And their righteousness is from Me," Says the Lord.
—Isaiah 54:17

WHO SHOULD SPEAK UP?

It is of utmost importance we as believers, realize that true transformation in our personal life, family life and in the life of our nation can only come about when we exercise our God-given power of the spoken word. We cannot afford to surrender and forfeit our God-given purpose, destiny and legacy, by refusing to use our God-given voices to stand up, speak up and fight for truth. No matter what circumstances or challenges we might be currently facing, we cannot expect spiritual victory while continuously piggybacking off the faith and anointing of our Christian friends, pastors, elders or family members.

Isaiah 54:17 is one of the Scripture verses most frequently used, when it comes to encountering personal attacks by the enemy. We love to quote the first part "No weapon formed against me shall prosper," yet we have a tendency to neglect the latter part which states, "And every tongue which rises against you in judgment you shall condemn." God requires that your voice and my voice be used during times of spiritual warfare. No believer is exempt from this command.

In Ecclesiastes 3:7, King Solomon writes that there is "...a time to keep silent and a time to speak." With this verse in mind, the question then becomes one of application: When exactly should one keep silent and when should one speak out, according to the will of God? This topic has been the source of much controversy among theologians and believers throughout the years. There are those who hold the mindset that "silence is golden" and that it is better to be seen than heard. On the opposing side, are those individuals who are persuaded that to keep silent, is to deny the very essence of their Christian faith and allegiance to the Word of God. After all, they argue, where would we be today if Jesus, the Apostle Paul, Martin Luther the Reformer, Abraham Lincoln and Martin Luther King Jr. shared the philosophy, that silence is more noble than speech? In seeking to resolve this tension, it is important to note that in Ecclesiastes 7:16-18 Solomon also warns us to refrain from all extremes. One thing that we must be careful about as believers is to maintain a biblically-informed balance in our actions, making sure the pendulum doesn't swing from one extreme to another. Knowing when to speak up and when not to speak, should be based on the leading of the Holy Spirit and a thorough assessment of the situation.

WHEN TO SPEAK UP?

Many of us are familiar with the Bible story of David and Goliath. One day while reading the account, I noticed something very interesting. 1 Samuel 17:16 states that Goliath the Philistine, the enemy of God, belligerently mocked the army of Israel, the people of God, twice a day for forty days and challenged them to engage him in battle. Yet according to verse 11, the people of Israel "...were dismayed and greatly afraid." Isn't it strange that Israel, which had the backing of Almighty God Himself, was silent while Goliath, the enemy of God, was the one boldly speaking up? You would have thought God's people would have been the ones issuing the challenge, knowing their God can do anything but fail! Regrettably, today we often see the same characteristic of fearful silence displayed in the Body of Christ. Many Christians have lost perspective of just how big their God is, while conjuring up all kinds of excuses for not taking a stand or speaking up for their biblical beliefs. There are a variety of creative excuses floating around Christian circles. For instance, some might say that since these are the last days before Jesus returns, there's no point in trying to change the world; it'll end soon enough. Others may assume they are not influential people and no one will listen to what they have to say. Many hold back due to fear of repercussions and others simply do not care. It is a tragedy to see believers sitting by silently, while every God hater, cult and demonic institution is boldly stepping up to the microphone of public opinion. Sadly, many Christians today prefer to take a passive approach towards defending their faith. A few months ago I was sitting with an acquaintance of mine, sharing my concern about the direction in which the church and our nation is headed. He expressed that he felt the only possible course of action was prayer, saying he felt that demonstrations, activism and things of this nature all seemed intolerant and condemning. He also noted that the Bible states that we as believers should always be ready at all times to "turn the other cheek." After a heated debate he asked me to clarify" when," in my opinion, would be the right time to stand up, speak out and confront the enemy. My reply was, "After you have turned all four cheeks and you don't have any more cheeks to turn, then it is time to go into the enemy's camp and take back what he has stolen from you!" We in America do not have any more cheeks to turn. Satan, our enemy, has taken over our nation, our churches and our families. Now is the time for the Body of Christ, to advance into enemy territory and reclaim all that is rightfully ours.

> Now is the time for the Body of Christ, to advance into enemy territory and reclaim all that is rightfully ours.

You may be wondering, "Adrian, when should a believer speak up?" I am glad you asked. First, one should speak up when encountering personal demonic attacks physically, mentally, financially or relationally. The Bible declares in 1 Peter 5:8 "Be sober, be vigilant; because your adversary the devil walks about like a roaring lion, seeking whom he may devour." Oftentimes the enemy will attack individually first, before attacking corporately. He will attack a husband knowing that the whole family will be affected because of his spiritual position and covering as head of the household. He will attack a pastor knowing that striking the shepherd will bring confusion, division and devastation to the sheep. If we speak up and fight back against individual attacks, we will then be able to stand in the gap and speak up for others being attacked by the enemy.

    Secondly, one should speak up when encountering a personal offense. Most Christians have adopted an unbiblical, unbalanced mindset concerning personal confrontation. Some choose to believe that overlooking every offense is a sign of spiritual humility and Christlikeness; others unwisely choose to confront every offense. Proverbs 19:11 states "A man's wisdom gives him patience; it is to his glory to overlook an offense." Yes, there are often times when an offense should be overlooked, but when one develops a continual pattern of offending, Jesus counsels us to confront the offender. Jesus stated in Matthew 18:15 "Moreover, if your brother sins against you, go and tell him his fault between you and him alone. If he hears you, you have gained your brother." When we choose to speak up in love and confront those who perpetually offend us, we are not only following the counsel of Jesus, but are guarding ourselves from the enemy's trap, of ensnaring us in a web of anger, bitterness and resentment. As an aside, there will be times, when it is our own pattern of giving offense, that must be addressed. In this case we must also speak up; Jesus admonishes us in Matthew 5:23-24 to go and be reconciled to the one we have offended. Spiritually mature individuals who are filled by the Holy Spirit, will strive for reconciliation and seek opportunities to rebuild broken bridges.

Thirdly, one should speak up for those who do not have a voice or the ability to defend themselves. Proverbs 31:8 commands us to "Speak up for those who cannot speak for themselves, for the rights of all who are destitute" (NIV). In America alone, 173 abortions are performed every hour, 3,288 abortions are performed every day and 1.2 million are performed yearly.[1] In Psalm 139:13-16 the Bible clearly illustrates God's overseeing supernatural involvement, prior to the physical conception of life. David said:

> "For You formed my inward parts; You covered me in my mother's womb. I will praise You, for I am fearfully and wonderfully made; Marvelous are Your works, And that my soul knows very well. My frame was not hidden from You, When I was made in secret, And skillfully wrought in the lowest parts of the earth. Your eyes saw my substance, being yet unformed. And in Your book they all were written, The days fashioned for me, When as yet there were none of them."

As followers of Jesus Christ, we must not be found silent on this critical issue. We are the voices, countless innocent children are counting on to speak life, rather than death, into existence.

As we enjoy freedom of religion in America, it is imperative we do not neglect nor forget those who are suffering for the cause of Christ. Paul writes in Hebrews 13:3 "Remember them that are in bonds, as bound with them; and them who suffer adversity, as being yourselves also in the body." It is crucial we believers use prayer and advocacy, to speak up for our brothers and sisters in Christ, who like never before, are being persecuted around the world.

Human trafficking is another global issue that urgently demands our attention. The 2010 Trafficking in Persons report by the U.S. Department of State estimates 12.3 million people are being held or trafficked in slavery worldwide and not even 1% of the victims have been identified to date.[2] Many of these individuals are women and children who were coerced or drugged into sexual slavery. This appalling practice is a direct assault by the enemy, upon those who bear God's image. As believers, we cannot pretend that modern day slavery does not exist; we must get involved and use our voice to stand against this atrocity.

> We are the voices, countless innocent children are counting on to speak life, rather than death, into existence.

Fourthly, Christians should speak up when encountering false doctrines, which do not align with the Word of God. In Jude 1:3-4 we read, "Beloved, while I was very diligent to write to you concerning our common salvation, I found it necessary to write to you exhorting you to contend earnestly for the faith which was once for all delivered to the saints. For certain men have crept in unnoticed, who long ago were marked out for this condemnation, ungodly men, who turn the grace of our God into lewdness and deny the only Lord God and our Lord Jesus Christ." Here Jude warns against and challenges believers to be on the alert for individuals who have become secret agents for satan. He reiterates what Peter said, when writing about false prophets who would infiltrate local bodies of believers and introduce God's people to demonic heresies. The Church in these last and final days can certainly not afford to be complacent, careless, nor lackadaisical, when it comes to upholding and defending biblical truth. 1 Peter 3:15 admonishes Christians, as defenders of the faith, to "...always be ready to give a defense to everyone who asks you a reason for the hope that is in you, with meekness and fear; having a good conscience, that when they defame you as evildoers, those who revile your good conduct in Christ may be ashamed." If we who call ourselves followers of Jesus Christ, are not willing to speak up and defend the living, inerrant and infallible Word of God, then we are justified in questioning the validity of our Christian conversion experience.

> If we who call ourselves followers of Jesus Christ, are not willing to speak up and defend the living, inerrant and infallible Word of God, then we are justified in questioning the validity of our Christian conversion experience.

Finally, Christians have a moral obligation to

speak up, whenever those placed in authority over them command them to behave in a manner that would require disobedience to God's Word. In spite of the fact that we are commanded in Scripture to respect and obey those in authority over us, we must remember our primary and foremost allegiance is to God and His Word. When King Nebuchadnezzar commanded Shadrach, Meshach and Abed-nego to worship his golden image, they "...answered and said to the king, 'O Nebuchadnezzar, we have no need to answer you in this matter. If that is the case, our God whom we serve is able to deliver us from the burning fiery furnace, and He will deliver us from your hand, O king. But if not, let it be known to you, O king, that we do not serve your gods, nor will we worship the gold image which you have set up'" (Daniel 3:16-18). Peter and John found themselves in a similar position when the Jewish leaders of Jerusalem gave them a stern warning not to speak or teach at all in the name of Jesus, to which they replied "Whether it is right in the sight of God to listen to you more than to God, you judge. For we cannot but speak the things which we have seen and heard" (Acts 4:19-20) and "...we ought to obey God rather than men" (Acts 5:29). Christians must not conform to an evil society, but must confront and oppose it when faced with a command or mandate that contradicts the Word of God.

WHEN NOT TO SPEAK UP?

In addition to Ecclesiastes 3:7, there are many other verses in the Bible that serve as illustrations of instances when "silence is golden." James 1:19 warns us to be "quick to hear, slow to speak, and slow to anger." Proverbs 17:28 states that "even a fool who keeps silent is considered wise; when he closes his lips, he is deemed intelligent" and warns us in Proverbs 11:12 that it is unwise to belittle our neighbor.

Furthermore, there are some other situations and times when one should be silent before speaking out. For example, one should be silent when dealing with one's own un-confessed sin. Luke 6:42 says "How can you say to your brother, 'Brother, let me remove the speck that is in your eye,' when you yourself do not see the plank that is in your own eye? Hypocrite! First remove the plank from your own eye, and then you will see clearly to remove the speck that is in your brother's eye." Every time we travel by plane, the flight attendant reminds us before takeoff, that if we experience a drop in cabin pressure during the flight, a mask will drop from the overhead compartment. He or she emphasizes that it is of utmost importance, to first place the mask on yourself and then help anyone around you who might need assistance. In essence, the attendant is saying you must first make sure you are saved before bringing salvation to others. Saving the world, the White House and the schoolhouse is a noble aspiration, but not at the expense of losing your house, due to a lack of personal repentance and transformation.

Secondly, one should be silent when one's motives for speaking up are rooted in ungodly anger. Psalm 4:4 admonishes us to "Be angry, and do not sin; meditate in your own hearts on your beds, and be silent." Anger is a powerful emotion. It can be used as a catalyst for great change; for example, William Wilberforce's anger over the injustice of slavery, brought about an abolishment of the slave trade in England.[3] It is not a sin to be angry, but it is a sin to be angry and act sinfully as a result.

Hatred, bitterness, revenge and self-justification are just some of the sins one may encounter while dealing with anger. None of these attributes will produce a pure motive for speaking out. Remember, one cannot be a conduit of salvation or transformation to a person he or she hates.

> It is not a sin to be angry, but it is a sin to be angry and act sinfully.

Thirdly, one should consider being silent when he or she is in the process of investigating a situation. One characteristic often overlooked in the life of Job, is that in addition to being a Godly man of character and integrity, he was also a very well-informed person. Job 29:16 states "I was a father to the poor and I searched out the case that I did not know." In today's society finding out the truth about a particular matter or issue can sometimes prove to be very difficult. If one is led by the Holy Spirit, to speak out on a particular matter, it is imperative they get their facts straight concerning the issue at hand. Sadly, many well-intentioned people embarrass themselves and the Kingdom of God by speaking out on issues based on conjecture and speculation. Proverbs

18:13 states "He who answers a matter before he hears it, it is his folly and shame to him." Keeping silent until we have all our cards on the table and have thoroughly investigated the case, will ensure bringing glory to the Kingdom of God, as a result of our speech.

Fourthly and finally, it is wise to keep silent until the Holy Spirit reveals the right time for one to speak out. If you say the right thing at the wrong time, the conversation will not produce the right results. As stated before, Ecclesiastes 3:7 states there is a time to be silent and a time to speak. Many people have the propensity to address an issue quickly, without waiting on the Lord to reveal to them the right time to confront it. They may even attempt to justify their brash actions, by saying that their thoughtless confrontation is "just part of their personality," or that in doing so they are being bold like Christ or the Apostle Paul. Unfortunately, individuals with this mentality only demonstrate their insecurity and self-centeredness. A spiritually mature individual will wait until he or she has received the green light from the Holy Spirit before speaking out. Timing is critical; you may not get a second chance, to say the right thing at the right time.

HOW TO SPEAK UP?

Now that we have established when and when not to speak up, it is imperative Christians know how to speak up. As stated before, it is possible for a person to speak the right thing, but doing so at the wrong time will result in little change and risks great damage. In the same manner, if an individual says the right thing at the right time, but does so in the wrong way, he or she will likely still reap a negative result.

The first step in knowing how to speak up, is admitting you truly might not know how to do so. James, the half-brother of Jesus, makes a very interesting statement about the tongue in James 3:8, stating, "But no man can tame the tongue; it is an unruly evil, full of deadly poison." In other words, the tongue cannot be controlled through fleshly means, nor by our own efforts alone. Only a Holy Spirit-filled person who regularly communicates with their Heavenly Father through prayer will be equipped with the wisdom to know how to speak up. In Isaiah 50:4, we find Jesus himself being instructed by God the Father on how He should speak. Isaiah 50:4 says, "The Lord God has given me the tongue of the learned, that I should know how to speak a word in season to him who is weary. He awakens me morning by morning, He awakens my ear to hear as the learned." If Jesus had to depend on His relationship with the Father to receive proper instruction on how He should speak, how much more should we do the same! It is foolish to expect Godly results while holding conversations guided by our carnal flesh, rather than the Holy Spirit.

    Secondly, one should examine the tone in which they speak up. The Apostle Paul wrote in Colossians 4:6, "Let your speech always be with grace, seasoned with salt, that you may know how you ought to answer each one." Luke 4:22 gives testimony to the manner in which Jesus communicated, while He was present physically here on earth, "So all bore witness to Him and marveled at the gracious words which proceeded out of His mouth." Furthermore, Luke 6:45 states that "A good man out of the good treasure of his heart brings forth good; and an evil man out of the evil treasure of his heart brings forth evil. For out of the abundance of the heart his mouth speaks." When a person is angry or harboring bitterness or resentment in their heart, they will often speak in an aggressive, confrontational tone. They may have a strong and valid point, but it's unlikely the person on the receiving end will be able to hear it, due to the manner in which the message is being conveyed! Proverbs 15:1 states that "a soft answer turns away wrath, but a harsh word stirs up anger." The tone in which one speaks will provide external evidence to one's true internal condition. This is why we must examine and purify ourselves of any pride, bitterness or selfish motive before speaking up. Since self-control is one of the Fruits of the Spirit, believers must always be filled with the Spirit of God to speak the truth in love. (Ephesians 4:15).

    Thirdly, we must speak up with an attitude of

> A soft answer turns away wrath, but a harsh word stirs up anger.
> **PROVERBS 15:1**

gentleness and humility. Even though Christians have a biblical and moral responsibility to speak up, we must never be found to have a sanctified superiority complex, rooted in a spirit of pride and arrogance. In Galatians 6:1-3 Paul writes, "Brethren, if a man is overtaken in any trespass, you who are spiritual restore such a one in a spirit of gentleness, considering yourself lest you also be tempted. Bear one another's burdens, and so fulfill the law of Christ. For if anyone thinks himself to be something, when he is nothing, he deceives himself."

On August 1, 2012, hundreds upon hundreds of people headed to Chick-fil-A to show their support of the restaurant's CEO Dan Cathy in his uncompromising, yet humble public stance for the traditional biblical definition of the family. Since I was in full agreement, I also wanted to demonstrate my support, by purchasing my lunch at the restaurant that particular day. Upon entering the facility, I immediately noticed a group of seven men wearing Christian T-shirts, who had apparently come together in a demonstration of solidarity. Overhearing their conversation, I noticed that they were not engaging in a God-honoring conversation about the matter at hand. While laughing and making ungodly and unkind jokes about the homosexual community, one had the arrogance to state that he wanted to come to Chick-fil-A everyday, because a "Chick-fil-A a day, will keep the homosexuals away." Many of the people in line, hearing his loud proclamation, laughed aloud and the man who had made the statement, grinned in apparent pride over his own wit. Following the group outside of the restaurant, I immediately and firmly rebuked them in love, strongly encouraging them to no longer wear their Christian T-shirts, if they had no intention of representing the Christ, portrayed on them. Chick-fil-A Day could have been a spark to start a revival in our nation; instead, it produced a riot due to many believers and individuals who did not fully understand what the Bible conveyed, when it says to speak the truth in love, or to be angry without sinning.

The Bible declares in Romans 3:23 that "all have sinned and fall short of the glory of God." Furthermore, 1 John 1:8 states, "If we say that we have no sin, we deceive ourselves, and the truth is not in us." It is imperative to remember both the saved and unsaved, will deal with sin until Jesus returns. Oftentimes, Christians have an ungodly habit of looking down their long religious noses, at those who struggle with different sins than they do, demonstrating a mindset of spiritual superiority over others. 1 John 1:8 is clear, even those of us who have accepted Jesus Christ as our personal Lord and Savior will not be sinless, but through the transforming power of the Holy Spirit will develop a pattern of sinning less. Whether speaking a little white lie, overeating or committing murder, all sin is grievous in the eyes of God. The consequences of sin may vary, but in the end both the sinner and the saint, are in continual need of the grace of God. We believers must continually be aware of our own tendency to sin, before we consider addressing the sins of others in an ungodly, arrogant, and prideful manner. Proverbs 11:2 says "When pride comes, then comes shame; but with the humble is wisdom." Meekness is not weakness when it comes to the Kingdom of God; meekness is power, under control. Verbal restoration and confrontation must be done in a spirit of gentleness and humility.

Fourthly, we must speak up confidently and boldly. Proverbs 28:1 declares, "The wicked flee when no one pursues, but the righteous are bold as a lion." While I was attending Bible college, I was required each week to participate in some form of evangelism. Evangelism during those days was somewhat different than the servant evangelism model we see today. In today's times, we think of creative ways to show God's love through practical ways, such as holding a block party or delivering Christmas gifts to families in need. Instead, we were trained in CWT (Christian Witness Training) and Evangelism Explosion by Dr. James Kennedy. Both of these evangelistic programs encouraged going door-to-door and engaging in personal, one-on-one interactions with individuals. One Tuesday evening, after making a few attempts to find anyone who would open their front door to me, I saw a man sitting in a rocking chair on his front porch. I made my way up the porch stairs and introduced myself. He said that his name was Melvin. Not knowing whether he was a Christian or not, I quickly began to recite my memorized Christian Witnessing Training outline. I had only uttered a few sentences of my speech when Melvin, with anger burning in his eyes, told me to "go to hell" and gave me instructions on how to get there. Being a little bit spiritually ticked off, but still full of passion for sharing my faith,

> Meekness is not weakness when it comes to the Kingdom of God; meekness is power, under control.

I pointed my finger at Melvin and in a stern voice said, "Melvin, I command you in the name of Jesus to repent of your sins and receive Jesus as your personal Lord and Savior. You are living in hell, and you don't want to die and go to hell." He might have tried to run me off, but I could see hurt and pain in his eyes and knew how badly he needed Jesus. The very next week I stopped by to see Melvin, but this time he was not on the porch in his rocking chair. A short, feeble, saddened lady opened the door after several knocks. As I introduced myself and began to inquire about Melvin's whereabouts, she quickly grabbed me by the arm and said, "You are the man, Melvin was talking about!" She revealed she was Melvin's wife and that she and her whole family prayed for years, for him to receive Jesus as his Lord and Savior. She mentioned, Melvin had frequently run off the Jehovah's Witness and the Mormons who came to his door, but was taken aback by the bold manner, in which I replied to his harsh attack. Three days after our first and only conversation, Melvin succumbed to a long battle with cancer. His wife, Eugene led him in the Sinner's Prayer the day before he passed. I will not know until the day I get to heaven, but I would like to believe, that the boldness God gave me the day I met Melvin, played a small, yet significant part in his decision, to receive Jesus as his personal Lord and Savior. God will often place a spirit of confidence and boldness in the voice of His children, because time is of the essence. Melvin only had three more days; I wonder how many more days you, your family, your friends and our nation have left. Pray for the courage to speak up now with confidence and boldness.

WHERE TO SPEAK UP?

Whether motivated by fear, anger or vindictiveness; Christians often communicate their hurts and frustrations to everyone, but the individual(s) directly involved in the situation. In my nineteen years of ministering I have seen firsthand, the irreparable damage that can result from this kind of behavior. Many times individuals guided by the wrong spirit, will use public prayer requests, as a means to voice their private frustrations. This in turn leads to gossip, division and confusion within the Body of Christ. Rather than praying for and confronting the offender privately, they chose to prey on the offender, by disclosing private matters in public. When we are prompted by the Holy Spirit, to confront an individual concerning their mindset, actions or behavior, we must begin the process, by speaking to them privately. Matthew 18:15 states, "Moreover if your brother sins against you, go and tell him his fault between you and him alone. If he hears you, you have gained your brother." In other words, we must first confront the individual who has offended us in a private, one-on-one setting. A face-to-face conversation in a neutral location, is the ideal scenario for such a conversation. If circumstances do not allow for a private meeting, I recommend having a phone conversation or writing a letter. However, neither of these methods should be used if a face-to-face conversation is possible. If the person is not willing to accept correction, then further action with a third party is warranted. Public action such as church discipline, should only come after multiple attempts at private reconciliation are made.

While we must be cautious in approaching instances of personal sin, there are important societal issues which we must speak out on publicly; these issues are too important to risk being silent about. Whether we are speaking up for the persecuted church, the cry of the unborn, the spiritual decline of our nation, or racial injustice, believers have a moral obligation to publically address these issues. Petitioning our Senators, Congressmen and women, using every form of media to raise awareness regarding various issues, and writing letters advocating for those being persecuted abroad, are just a few ways we can publicly raise our voices. Another means of lending a voice, is volunteering at agencies which support and share the same passion, as you do, about a particular cause. Also, holding personal conversations with your coworkers, neighbors, and friends may be another way of bringing awareness to issues demanding attention. Social movements and change are brought about, when many small voices unite to create a loud voice regarding a single issue. After identifying a few causes you want to stand up and speak out about, commit to praying daily concerning those issues. Continue to research what is already being done both locally and nationally, and find a way to join those individuals and organizations, who are already speaking up for the same causes.

COST OF SPEAKING UP

The Bible warns us that speaking on behalf of righteousness often carries a high price tag. It may cost us our livelihoods, our friends, our family, even our lives. Jesus said in Mark 8:34-38,

> "Whoever desires to come after Me, let him deny himself, and take up his cross, and follow Me. For whoever desires to save his life will lose it, but whoever loses his life for My sake and the gospel's will save it. For what will it profit a man if he gains the whole world, and loses his own soul? Or what will a man give in exchange for his soul? For whoever is ashamed of Me and My words in this adulterous and sinful generation, of him the Son of Man also will be ashamed when He comes in the glory of His Father with the holy angels."

Whether we choose to speak up or not, there is a price to be paid. Silence has a voice of its own. Martin Niemoller, a German pastor who initially embraced Hitler and was later imprisoned himself, for opposing the Nazi regime during the Holocaust stated in deep regret:

> In Germany they came first for the Communists, and I didn't speak up because I wasn't a Communist. They came for the Jews, and I didn't speak up because I wasn't a Jew. Then they came for the trade unionists, and I didn't speak up because I wasn't a trade unionist. Then they came for the

Catholics, and I didn't speak up because I was Protestant. Then they came for me, and by that time no one was left to speak up.[4]

When we choose to willfully disobey, the urgings of the Holy Spirit to speak up, it will negatively affect not only our destiny, but our legacy as well. It was Martin Luther King, Jr. who said "In the end, we will remember not the words of our enemies, but the silence of our friends." [5] The greatest consequence of neglecting to speak up, is not the remorse or guilt we might encounter, but as Jesus states in Matthew 10:33, "...whoever denies Me before men, him I will also deny before My Father who is in heaven." It is one thing to be rejected by our governmental leaders, peers, family and friends but to be denied by our Lord and Savior Jesus Christ is to separate ourselves from God Himself for all eternity.

> In the end, we will remember not the words of our enemies, but the silence of our friends.
> - **MARTIN LUTHER KING, JR.**

It is understandably frightening to speak up for God in a truth-resistant culture, but we are not the first generation, called to radical Christianity. In Revelation 2:8-11 John writes,

> *"And to the angel of the church in Smyrna write, These things says the First and the Last, who was dead, and came to life: ' I know your works, tribulation, and poverty (but you are rich); and I know the blasphemy of those who say they are Jews and*

are not, but are a synagogue of satan. Do not fear any of those things which you are about to suffer. Indeed, the devil is about to throw some of you into prison, that you may be tested, and you will have tribulation ten days. Be faithful until death, and I will give you the crown of life. He who has an ear, let him hear what the Spirit says to the churches. He who overcomes shall not be hurt by the second death."

The pastor of the church of Smyrna at the time was a man by the name of Polycarp. Knowing the intense amount of suffering and persecution the church was encountering, John wrote this letter to encourage them. In 156 A.D., the Roman emperor Diocletian demanded Christians declare him to be God and burn incense in the temple on his behalf. Anyone who did not practice this mandate was considered to be a traitor to their country and disloyal to their government. Many Christians refused to obey and as a result were tortured, boiled in oil, crucified or thrown to the lions. In an effort to eliminate the Christians in Smyrna, the authorities arrested Polycarp, the pastor of the local church. When the chief magistrate asked him, "What harm is it to say Lord Caesar?!" Polycarp responded "Eighty and six years have I served Him and He never did me any harm; how then can I blaspheme my King and my Savior, who hath saved me?" Polycarp was then taken inside the stadium where he was to be executed in front

> Your legacy and eternal destiny resides in your voice!

of an angry crowd. After being threatened to be fed to the hungry lions and given another opportunity to deny Christ, he replied, "Let them come, for my purpose is unchangeable." Since the ruling authorities could not persuade him to blaspheme against the Lord by threatening to throw him to the lions, they then threatened him with being burned alive at the stake. Polycarp replied "Thou threatenest me with fire which will perhaps burn for an hour and then soon go out; but thou art ignorant of the fire of the future judgment of God which is prepared and reserved for the everlasting punishment and torment of the ungodly. But why do you delay? Bring on the beasts, or the fire, or whatever thou mayest choose: thou shalt not, by either of them, move me to deny Christ, my Lord and Savior." The magistrate then commanded that Polycarp be burned. As he was about to be set on fire, Polycarp looked toward heaven and prayed:

> *O Father...I thank thee that thou didst call me to this day and hour, and hast counted me worthy that I may have my part and place among the number of the holy martyrs. I pray thee, O Lord, that thou wouldst this day receive me, as a fat offering among the number of thy holy martyrs. I thank and praise thee, above other men and honor thy holy name, through Jesus Christ, thy well-beloved Son, the eternal High Priest, unto whom, with thee and the Holy Ghost, be the glory, now and forever. Amen.*

After he ended his prayer, the officers lit the fire. When the mob of people saw the flames encircling his body were not consuming him, they cried out to the executioner to pierce his body with a sword. Even after he had died the authorities would not release his body for burial until all of his flesh had burned and there was nothing left but his bones.[6] Polycarp was a fearless, faithful and uncompromising leader and witness for Jesus Christ to the Christian community in Smyrna, and as a result he left a legacy not only of how one should live for Christ, but die for Him as well. Your legacy and your eternal destiny resides in the power of your voice! Everyone who has accepted Jesus as their Lord and Savior has a price to pay and a cross to carry. Jesus said in Matthew 10:38-39, "And he who does not take his cross and follow after Me is not worthy of Me. He who finds his life will lose it, and he who loses his life for My sake will find it." Yes, there is a high price to pay for those who are willing to stand up and speak up for Christ, but there is an even greater price to pay, for those who don't. Either way a price has to be paid. Just make sure whatever price you choose to pay, is the one that yields an eternal return on your investment.

> There is a high price to pay for those who are willing to stand up and speak up for Christ, but there is an even greater price to pay, for those who don't.

THE
POWER
IS IN
YOUR
VOICE

CONCLUSION

CONCLUSION

The Body of Christ can no longer allow society to portray us as timid, cowardly individuals, who hide behind their Bibles and church pews. Like Joshua, not only must we choose this day whom we will serve, but we must also be willing to boldly and publicly declare that as for me and my house, we will serve the Lord. Satan, knowing the power of life and death is in the tongue (Proverbs 18:21), will continuously try to silence our voice with a spirit of fear and timidity. In 2 Timothy 1:7, Paul writes, "For God has not given us a spirit of fear, but of power and of love and of a sound mind." This verse clearly indicates that a spirit of fear comes directly from the devil. This is why it is so important to be filled with the Holy Spirit, for being filled with the Holy Spirit is the only way we can defeat the spirit of fear. Fear and faith can never coexist, as they are not of the same spirit. Acts 4:31 gives us a great illustration of what happens when believers are filled with the Holy Spirit: "And when they had prayed, the place where they were assembled together was shaken; and they were all filled with the Holy Spirit, and they spoke the word of God with boldness." This verse illustrates that speaking with boldness is a direct result of being filled with the Holy Spirit. As followers of Jesus Christ, we must understand that spiritual confidence, is not the same as worldly arrogance. Paul writes in Philippians 1:6, "...being confident of this very thing, that He who has begun a good work in you will complete it until the day of Jesus Christ." If Hitler, under the power of satan and all of his demons could boldly raise his voice and tragically bring death to 6 million Jews, I wonder how much life, those of us who are filled with the Holy Spirit of God, could bring if we confidently raised our voices and boldly spoke up for the cause of Christ. Pray for the Holy Spirit to give you a confident, bold and wise voice to address the issues we are facing today and watch God use your voice to bring healing, restoration and change to a hurting and dying world.

> God has always used imperfect, common, ordinary people to accomplish His will.

    If there has ever been a time for God's people to stand up and speak up, it is now! In Isaiah 58:1, God instructed the prophet Isaiah to "Cry aloud, spare not; Lift up your voice like a trumpet." No, we might not have all of our spiritual t's crossed or i's dotted, but God has always used imperfect, common, ordinary people to accomplish His will. If you see yourself as a less than perfect individual who is not qualified to be used by God, you are the primary candidate the Lord is looking to use in building

CONCLUSION

up His Kingdom. Paul writes in 1 Corinthians 1:26-29,

> *"For you see your calling, brethren, that not many wise according to the flesh, not many mighty, not many noble, are called. But God has chosen the foolish things of the world to put to shame the wise, and God has chosen the weak things of the world to put to shame the things which are mighty; and the base things of the world and the things which are despised God has chosen, and the things which are not, to bring to nothing the things that are, that no flesh should glory in His presence."*

The Bible is full of examples of how God used the most unlikely people to accomplish His purpose. Jacob was a trickster and a con-man, but God refers to Himself as the God of Abraham, Isaac and Jacob. David was an adulterer and a murderer, but God still called him a man after His own heart. Rahab was a prostitute running the red light district on 5th and 9th, but she is mentioned not only in the hall of faith in the book of Hebrews, but also in the genealogy of Jesus. Abraham was a liar, but God allowed him to be the father of all nations. Peter had a cussing problem and denied Jesus three times, but preached the first sermon on the day of Pentecost where three thousand people responded to the invitation. Moses was a murderer and had a stuttering problem, but God used him to deliver over one million Israelites out from the oppression of Egypt. Mary Magdalene had seven demons cast out of her, but was the first person to see Jesus after His resurrection. As it has been often said, "God does not call the qualified, but qualifies the called." He is not looking for perfect people, just people who are willing to be perfected through the power of the Holy Spirit. Still, there might be some of you who might be thinking "Adrian, unlike you I cannot boldly declare that I've got martyr's blood running through my veins. I did not inherit a family legacy of persecution and martyrdom." Consider this: if Jesus Christ is your personal Lord and Savior, I challenge you to go back and review your spiritual family tree and history. There you will find that you are a son or daughter of your Heavenly Father Jesus Christ. The Bible says in John 1:12 "But, to as many received Him, to them He gave the right to become children of God, even to those who believe in His Name." Furthermore, Isaiah 53:5 gives us further historical insight concerning our Heavenly Father stating, "But He was wounded for our transgressions, He was bruised for our iniquities; The chastisement for our peace was upon Him, And by His stripes we are healed." In 1912 evangelist George Bennard wrote about it this way:

> On a hill far away stood an old rugged cross,
> the emblem of suffering and shame;
> and I love that old cross where the dearest and best
> for a world of lost sinners was slain.
> So I'll cherish the old rugged cross,
> till my trophies at last I lay down;

CONCLUSION

*I will cling to the old rugged cross,
and exchange it someday for a crown.*[1]

If you can confidently and boldly testify that your sins have been washed by the shed blood of Jesus Christ, you also have martyr's blood running through your veins. Jesus not only died for you, but defeated death and arose on the third day from the grave, with all power in His hand to ensure His children can obtain victory in life and in death. Therefore, since you have the same power working within you that raised Christ from the dead (Romans 8:11), I challenge you who have been saved, you who have been washed in the blood of the Lamb, you who have been Spirit-filled, you who have been given the power and authority to bind and loose things on earth and in heaven, open up your mouth and Tell Hell, "No!"

When you think God does not love you
Tell Hell, "No!"

When the devil tries to convince you that you have no purpose or destiny
Tell Hell, "No!"

When you think you have fallen so deep in sin that God can't pull you out
Tell Hell, "No!"

When you think God has abandoned or forsaken you
Tell Hell, "No!"

When you've lost all hope and you think tomorrow will not be any better than today
Tell Hell, "No!"

When the demonic spirit of suicide tries to overtake you
Tell Hell, "No!"

When the doctor tells you, your health condition is incurable
Tell Hell, "No!"

When the devil tells you, your children or grandchildren will never be saved
Tell Hell, "No!"

When the enemy wants you to succumb to peer pressure
Tell Hell, "No!"

When the devil tempts you to give up your virginity
Tell Hell, "No!"

When the devil tries to convince you, you will never marry a godly mate
Tell Hell, "No!"

When the bank says they will foreclose on your house
Tell Hell, "No!"

CONCLUSION

When the devil tells you that you will never own your own business

Tell Hell, "No!"

When our nation's leaders try to change the biblical definition of the family and marriage

Tell Hell, "No!"

When our judicial system wants to strip the courthouse of the Ten Commandments

Tell Hell, "No!"

When our children are told they cannot pray in school

Tell Hell, "No!"

When the devil tells you to shut up, sit down and be quiet

Tell Hell, "No!"

THE POWER IS IN YOUR VOICE

THE POWER IS IN YOUR VOICE

APPENDIX 1
SCRIPTURES
TABLE OF CONTENTS

SPIRITUAL FOUNDATIONS

GOD'S PLAN OF SALVATION	88
GOD'S FORGIVENESS	89
GOD'S EVERLASTING LOVE	89
GOD'S PLAN FOR YOU	90
GOD'S GUIDANCE	90
GOD'S WORD	91
SATAN & SPIRITUAL WARFARE	91

BIBLICAL APPLICATIONS FOR LIFE

ABANDONMENT	92
ABORTION	92

ANGER..93

ANXIETY & WORRY...93

CARING FOR YOUR BODY..................................94

CONDEMNATION..94

CONFUSION...95

DEPRESSION..95

ENEMIES 96

FAITH...96

FEAR..97

FINANCES..97

FORGIVING OTHERS..99

GIVING UP & QUITTING...................................99

GLUTTONY & DRUNKENNESS 100

GOSSIP..100

GREED & WORLDLINESS................................101

GRIEF..101

HATE & UNLOVING SPIRIT............................102

HOMOSEXUALITY..103

LETTING GO OF THE PAST............................104

LUST & IMMORALITY...104

MARRIAGE..105

PATIENCE..106

PEACE..107

- PRAYER...107
- PRIDE...108
- RENEWING YOUR MIND.......................................108
- RESTORATION..109
- SICKNESS...109
- SUICIDE & DEATH..110
- TEMPTATION..110
- TRIALS & PERSECUTION.....................................111
- WEARINESS..111
- WITCHCRAFT & SORCERY 112
- WISDOM...113

APPENDIX 1: SCRIPTURES

SPIRITUAL FOUNDATIONS

GOD'S PLAN OF SALVATION
(John 3:16; Ephesians 2:8-9; Acts 16:30-31)

ROMANS 3:23
For all have sinned and fall short of the glory of God.

ROMANS 6:23
For the wages of sin is death, but the gift of God is eternal life in Christ Jesus our Lord.

ROMANS 5:8
But God demonstrates His own love toward us, in that while we were yet sinners, Christ died for us.

APPENDIX 1

GOD'S FORGIVENESS
(Isaiah 43:25; John 5:24; Psalms 103:12)

1 JOHN 1:9
If we confess our sins, He is faithful and just to forgive us our sins and to cleanse us from all unrighteousness.

2 CORINTHIANS 5:17
Therefore, if anyone is in Christ, he is a new creation; old things have passed away; behold, all things have become new.

GOD'S EVERLASTING LOVE
(1 John 4:18; Psalm 36:5; Psalm 103:11)

ROMANS 8:35
Who shall separate us from the love of Christ? Shall tribulation, or distress, or persecution, or famine, or nakedness, or peril, or sword?

ROMANS 8:37-39
Yet in all these things we are more than conquerors through Him who loved us. For I am persuaded that neither death nor life, nor angels nor principalities nor powers, nor things present nor things to come, nor height nor depth, nor any other created thing, shall be able to separate us from the love of God which is in Christ Jesus our Lord.

GOD'S PLAN FOR YOU
(Philippians 1:6; Ephesians 2:10; Jeremiah 1:5)

1 CORINTHIANS 2:9
But as it is written:
"Eye has not seen, nor ear heard,
Nor have entered into the heart of man
The things which God has prepared for those who love Him."

JEREMIAH 29:11
For I know the thoughts that I think toward you, says the Lord, thoughts of peace and not of evil, to give you a future and a hope.

GOD'S GUIDANCE
(Psalms 23:1-6; Psalm 32:8; Matthew 7:7-11)

PROVERBS 3:5-6
Trust in the Lord with all your heart,
And lean not on your own understanding;
In all your ways acknowledge Him,
And He shall direct your paths.

PSALM 119:105
Your word is a lamp to my feet
And a light to my path.

APPENDIX 1

GOD'S WORD
(Hebrews 4:12; Isaiah 55:11; Mark 13:31)

2 TIMOTHY 3:16
All Scripture is given by inspiration of God, and is profitable for doctrine, for reproof, for correction, for instruction in righteousness.

2 PETER 1:20-21
Knowing this first, that no prophecy of Scripture is of any private interpretation, for prophecy never came by the will of man, but holy men of God spoke as they were moved by the Holy Spirit.

SATAN & SPIRITUAL WARFARE
(1 John 4:1-4; Corinthians 10:3-5; Isaiah 54:17)

1 PETER 5:8-9
Be sober, be vigilant; because your adversary the devil walks about like a roaring lion, seeking whom he may devour. Resist him, steadfast in the faith, knowing that the same sufferings are experienced by your brotherhood in the world.

EPHESIANS 6:10-12
Finally, my brethren, be strong in the Lord and in the power of His might. Put on the whole armor of God, that you may be able to stand against the wiles of the devil. For we do not wrestle against flesh and blood, but against principalities, against powers, against the rulers of the darkness of this age, against spiritual hosts of wickedness in the heavenly places.

BIBLICAL APPLICATIONS FOR LIFE

ABANDONMENT
(Psalm 34:18; Isaiah 43:2; Psalm 27:10)

HEBREWS 13:5
I will never leave you or forsake you.

ROMANS 8:38-39
For I am persuaded that neither death nor life, nor angels nor principalities nor powers, nor things present nor things to come, nor height nor depth, nor any other created thing, shall be able to separate us from the love of God which is in Christ Jesus our Lord.

ABORTION
(Exodus 20:13; Deuteronomy 27:25; Deuteronomy 30:19)

JEREMIAH 1:5
Before I formed you in the womb I knew you,
before you were born I sanctified you.
I ordained you a prophet to the nations.

PSALM 139:13-14
For you created my inmost being, you knit me together in my mother's womb. I praise you because I am fearfully and wonderfully made.

APPENDIX 1

ANGER
(Proverbs 16:32; Ephesians 4:31-32; Proverbs 14:29)

EPHESIANS 4:26
Be angry, and do not sin, do not let the sun go down on your wrath.

JAMES 1:19-20
So then, my beloved brethren, let every man be swift to hear, slow to speak, slow to wrath; for the wrath of man does not produce the righteousness of God.

ANXIETY & WORRY
(Philippians 4:6; Matthew 6:31-34; John 14:27)

MATTHEW 6:25-27
Therefore I tell you, do not be anxious about your life, what you will eat or what you will drink, nor about your body, what you will put on. Is not life more than food, and the body more than clothing? Look at the birds of the air: they neither sow nor reap nor gather into barns, and yet your heavenly Father feeds them. Are you not of more value than they? And which of you by being anxious can add a single hour to his span of life?

1 PETER 5:7
Cast all your care upon Him, for He cares for you.

CARING FOR YOUR BODY
(Proverbs 17:22; 1 Corinthians 3:17; 1 Corinthians 10:31)

1 CORINTHIANS 6: 19-20
Or do you not know that your body is the temple of the Holy Spirit who is in you, whom you have from God, and you are not your own? For you were bought at a price; therefore glorify God in your body and in your spirit, which are God's.

3 JOHN 1:2
Beloved, I pray that you may prosper in all things and be in health, just as your soul prospers.

CONDEMNATION
(John 8:10-11; Romans 8:34; Psalm 34:21-22)

ROMANS 8:1
There is therefore now no condemnation to those who are in Christ Jesus, who do not walk according to the flesh, but according to the Spirit.

JOHN 3:17-18
For God did not send His Son into the world to condemn the world, but that the world through Him might be saved. "He who believes in Him is not condemned; but he who does not believe is condemned already, because he has not believed in the name of the only begotten Son of God.

CONFUSION
(1 John 4:1; John 16:13; 1 Corinthians 14:40)

1 CORINTHIANS 14:33
For God is not the author of confusion but of peace, as in all the churches of the saints.

JAMES 3:16-18
For where envy and self-seeking exist, confusion and every evil thing are there. But the wisdom that is from above is first pure, then peaceable, gentle, willing to yield, full of mercy and good fruits, without partiality and without hypocrisy. Now the fruit of righteousness is sown in peace by those who make peace.

DEPRESSION
(Psalm 42:5; Psalm 55:22; 2 Corinthians1:3-4; Isaiah 40:31)

PSALM 34:17-19
The righteous cry out, and the Lord hears,
And delivers them out of all their troubles.
The Lord is near to those who have a broken heart,
And saves such as have a contrite spirit.
Many are the afflictions of the righteous,
But the Lord delivers him out of them all.

PSALM 30:5
Weeping may endure for a night,
But joy comes in the morning.

ENEMIES
(Romans 12:19; Proverbs 25:21-22; Romans 8:31)

PSALM 23:5
You prepare a table before me in the presence of my enemies;
You anoint my head with oil;
My cup runs over.

MATTHEW 5:44
But I say to you, love your enemies, bless those who curse you, do good to those who hate you, and pray for those who spitefully use you and persecute you.

FAITH
(Hebrews 11:1; Hebrews 11:6; Romans 1:17; 2 Corinthians 5:7)

MARK 11:22-24
So Jesus answered and said to them, "Have faith in God. For assuredly, I say to you, whoever says to this mountain, 'Be removed and be cast into the sea,' and does not doubt in his heart, but believes that those things he says will be done, he will have whatever he says. Therefore I say to you, whatever things you ask when you pray, believe that you receive them, and you will have them.

ROMANS 10:17
So then faith comes by hearing, and hearing by the word of God.

APPENDIX 1

FEAR
(Psalm 91:4-5; Psalm 91:11; Proverbs 3:25-26

2 TIMOTHY 1:7
For God has not given us a spirit of fear, but of power and of love and of a sound mind.

PSALM 27:1-3
The Lord is my light and my salvation;
Whom shall I fear?
The Lord is the strength of my life;
Of whom shall I be afraid?
When the wicked came against me
To eat up my flesh,
My enemies and foes,
They stumbled and fell.
Though an army may encamp against me,
My heart shall not fear;
Though war may rise against me,
In this I will be confident.

FINANCES
(Deuteronomy 28:2-8; Psalm 37:25; 2 Corinthians 9:6-8; Proverbs 13:22)

PHILIPPIANS 4:19
And my God shall supply all your need according to His riches in glory by Christ Jesus.

TELL HELL NO

MALACHI 3:8-11
"Will a man rob God?
Yet you have robbed Me!
But you say,
'In what way have we robbed You?'
In tithes and offerings.
You are cursed with a curse,
For you have robbed Me,
Even this whole nation.
Bring all the tithes into the storehouse,
That there may be food in My house,
And try Me now in this,"
Says the Lord of hosts,
"If I will not open for you the windows of heaven
And pour out for you such blessing
That there will not be room enough to receive it.
"And I will rebuke the devourer for your sakes,
So that he will not destroy the fruit of your ground,
Nor shall the vine fail to bear fruit for you in the field,"
Says the Lord of hosts;

FORGIVING OTHERS
(Matthew 18:21-22; Luke 6:37; Proverbs 19:11)

MATTHEW 6:14-15
For if you forgive men their trespasses, your heavenly Father will also forgive you But if you do not forgive men their trespasses, neither will your Father forgive your trespasses.

EPHESIANS 4:31-32
Let all bitterness, wrath, anger, clamor, and evil speaking be put away from you, with all malice. And be kind to one another, tenderhearted, forgiving one another, even as God in Christ forgave you.

GIVING UP & QUITTING
(Philippians 1:6; Matthew 11:28; 2 Chronicles 15:7)

PHILIPPIANS 4:13
I can do all things through Christ who strengthens me.

GALATIANS 6:9
And let us not grow weary while doing good, for in due season we shall reap if we do not lose heart.

GLUTTONY & DRUNKENNESS
(1 Corinthians 6:19-20; Proverbs 20:1; Romans 12:1)

PROVERBS 23:20-21
Do not mix with winebibbers, or with gluttonous eaters of meat; For the drunkard and the glutton will come to poverty,
And drowsiness will clothe a man with rags.

EPHESIANS 5:18
And do not get drunk with wine, for that is dissipation, but be filled with the Holy Spirit.

GOSSIP
(Matthew 12:36, Proverbs 6:16-19, Titus 3:2)

PROVERBS 16:28
A dishonest man spreads strife, and a whisperer separates close friends.

2 TIMOTHY 2:16
But avoid irreverent babble, for it will lead people into more and more ungodliness.

GREED & WORLDLINESS
(Luke 12:15; 1 Timothy 6:10; Proverbs 11:24)

MARK 8:36
For what will it profit a man if he gains the whole world, and loses his own soul?

1 JOHN 2: 15-17
Do not love the world or the things in the world. If anyone loves the world, the love of the Father is not in him. For all that is in the world—the lust of the eyes, and the pride of life—is not of the Father but is of the world. And the world is passing away, and the lust of it; but he who does the will of the God abides forever.

GRIEF
(Matthew 5:4; 1 Corinthians 15:55-57; Revelation 21:4)

1 THESSALONIANS 4:13-14
But I do not want you to be ignorant, brethren, concerning those who have fallen asleep, lest you sorrow as others who have no hope. For if we believe that Jesus died and rose again, even so God will bring with Him those who sleep in Jesus.

2 CORINTHIANS 1:3-4
Blessed be the God and Father of our Lord Jesus Christ, the Father of mercies and God of all comfort, who comforts us in all our tribulation, that we may be able to comfort those who are in any trouble, with the comfort with which we ourselves are comforted by God.

HATE & UNLOVING SPIRIT
(1 JOHN 3:15; LUKE 10:27; MATTHEW 5:23-26)

1 JOHN 4:7-12
Beloved, let us love one another, for love is of God; and everyone who loves is born of God and knows God. He who does not love does not know God, for God is love. In this the love of God was manifested toward us, that God has sent His only begotten Son into the world, that we might live through Him. In this is love, not that we loved God, but that He loved us and sent His Son to be the propitiation for our sins. Beloved, if God so loved us, we also ought to love one another. No one has seen God at any time. If we love one another, God abides in us, and His love has been perfected in us.

1 CORINTHIANS 13:1-3
Though I speak with the tongues of men and of angels, but have not love, I have become sounding brass or a clanging cymbal. And though I have the gift of prophecy, and understand all mysteries and all knowledge, and though I have all faith, so that I could remove mountains, but have not love, I am nothing. And though I bestow all my goods to feed the poor, and though I give my body to be burned, but have not love, it profits me nothing.

APPENDIX 1

HOMOSEXUALITY
(1 Corinthians 6:9-10; Leviticus 20:13; Genesis 13:13)

ROMANS 1:18-27
For the wrath of God is revealed from heaven against all ungodliness and unrighteousness of men, who suppress the truth in unrighteousness, because hat may be known of God is manifest in them, for God has shown it to them. For since the creation of the world His invisible attributes are clearly seen, being understood by the things that are made, even His eternal power and Godhead, so that they are without excuse, because, although they knew God, they did not glorify Him as God, nor were thankful, but became futile in their thoughts, and their foolish hearts were darkened. Professing to be wise, they became fools, and changed the glory of the incorruptible God into an image made like corruptible man—and birds and four-footed animals and creeping things. Therefore God also gave them up to uncleanness, in the lusts of their hearts, to dishonor their bodies among themselves, who exchanged the truth of God for the lie, and worshiped and served the creature rather than the Creator, who is blessed forever. Amen. For this reason God gave them up to vile passions. For even their women exchanged the natural use for what is against nature. Likewise also the men, leaving the natural use of the woman, burned in their lust for one another, men with men committing what is shameful, and receiving in themselves the penalty of their error which was due.

LEVITICUS 18:22
You shall not lie with a male as with a woman. It is an abomination.

LETTING GO OF THE PAST
(2 Corinthians 5:17-18; Galatians 2:20; 1 John 1:9)

PHILIPPIANS 3:13-14
Brethren, I do not count myself to have apprehended; but one thing I do, forgetting those things which are behind and reaching forward to those things which are ahead, I press toward the goal for the prize of the upward call of God in Christ Jesus.

ISAIAH 43:18-19
"Do not remember the former things,
Nor consider the things of old.
Behold, I will do a new thing,
Now it shall spring forth;
Shall you not know it?
I will even make a road in the wilderness
And rivers in the desert.

LUST & IMMORALITY
(Galatians 5:16-26; 1 Corinthians 6:18; 2 Timothy 2:22)

MATTHEW 5:27-28
"You have heard that it was said to those of old, 'You shall not commit adultery.' But I say to you that whoever looks at a woman to lust for her has already committed adultery with her in his heart.

APPENDIX 1

1 JOHN 2: 15-17
Do not love the world or the things in the world. If anyone loves the world, the love of hte Father is not in him. For all that is in the world—the lust of the flesh, the lust of the eyes, and the pride of life—is not of the Father but is of the world. And the world is passing away, and the lust of it; but he who does the will of God abides forever.

MARRIAGE
(Joshua 24:15; 1 Peter 3:1-7; Proverbs 31)

EPHESIANS 5:21-33
...submitting to one another in the fear of God. Wives, submit to your own husbands, as to the Lord. For the husband is head of the wife, as also Christ is head of the church; and He is the Savior of the body. Therefore, just as the church is subject to Christ, so let the wives be to their own husbands in everything. Husbands, love your wives, just as Christ also loved the church and gave Himself for her, that He might sanctify and cleanse her with the washing of water by the word, that He might present her to Himself a glorious church, not having spot or wrinkle or any such thing, but that she should be holy and without blemish. So husbands ought to love their own wives as their own bodies; he who loves his wife loves himself. For no one ever hated his own flesh, but nourishes and cherishes it, just as the Lord does the church. For we are members of His body, of His flesh and of His bones. "For this reason a man shall leave his father and mother and be joined to his wife, and the two shall become one flesh."

This is a great mystery, but I speak concerning Christ and the church. Nevertheless let each one of you in particular so love his own wife as himself, and let the wife see that she respects her husband.

1 CORINTHIANS 13:4-7
Love suffers long and is kind; love does not envy; love does not parade itself, is not puffed up; does not behave rudely, does not seek its own, is not provoked, thinks no evil; does not rejoice in iniquity, but rejoices in the truth; bears all things, believes all things, hopes all things, endures all things.
Love never fails.

PATIENCE
(Psalm 40:1; 1 Corinthians 13:4; Psalm 40:1-3)

JAMES 1:4
But let patience have its perfect work, that you may be perfect and complete, lacking nothing.

ISAIAH 40:31
But those who wait on the Lord
Shall renew their strength;
They shall mount up with wings like eagles,
They shall run and not be weary,
They shall walk and not faint.

APPENDIX 1

PEACE
(Romans 14:17-19; John 14:27; Galatians 5:22)

ISAIAH 26:3
You will keep him in perfect peace,
Whose mind is stayed on You,
Because he trusts in You.

PHILIPPIANS 4:6-7
Be anxious for nothing, but in everything by prayer and supplication, with thanksgiving, let your requests be made known to God; and the peace of God, which surpasses all understanding, will guard your hearts and minds through Christ Jesus.

PRAYER
(Jeremiah 33:3; Romans 8:26; Matthew 6:9-13)

2 CHRONICLES 7:14
If My people who are called by My name will humble themselves, and pray and seek My face, and turn from their wicked ways, then I will hear from heaven, and will forgive their sin and heal their land.

PHILIPPIANS 4:6
Be anxious for nothing, but in everything by prayer and supplication, with thanksgiving, let your requests be made known to God.

PRIDE
(Proverbs 11:2; Proverbs 29:23; Deuteronomy 8:11-14)

PROVERBS 16:18
Pride goes before destruction, and a haughty spirit before a fall.

ROMANS 12:3
For I say, through the grace given to me, to everyone who is among you, not to think of himself more highly than he ought to think, but to think soberly, as God has dealt to each one a measure of faith.

RENEWING THE MIND
(Philippians 2:5; 2 Corinthians 10:3-5; Romans 8:6)

ROMANS 12:2
And do not be conformed to this world, but be transformed by the renewing of your mind, that you may prove what is that good and acceptable and perfect will of God.

PHILIPPIANS 4:8
Finally, brethren, whatever things are true, whatever things are noble, whatever things are just, whatever things are pure, whatever things are lovely, whatever things are of good report, if there is any virtue and if there is anything praiseworthy—meditate on these things.

APPENDIX 1

RESTORATION
(Isaiah 61:7; Job 42:10; Psalm 23:1-6)

MATTHEW 19:29
And everyone who has left houses or brothers or sisters or father or mother or wife or children or lands, for My name's sake, shall receive a hundredfold, and inherit eternal life.

JOEL 2:25
So I will restore to you the years that the swarming locust has eaten,
The crawling locust,
The consuming locust,
And the chewing locust,
My great army which I sent among you.

SICKNESS
(James 5:14-15; Psalm 107:20; 3 John 1:2)

1 PETER 2:24
He who bore our sins in His own body on the tree, that we, having died to sins, might live for righteousness by whose stripes you were healed.

EXODUS 15:26
"If you diligently heed the voice of the Lord your God and do what is right in His sight, give ear to His commandments and keep all His statutes, I will put none of the diseases on you which I have brought on the Egyptians. For I am the Lord who heals you."

SUICIDE & DEATH
(Ecclesiastes 7:17; 1 Corinthians 3:17; Exodus 20:13)

JOHN 10:10
The thief does not come except to steal, and to kill, and to destroy. I have come that they may have life, and that they may have it more abundantly.

PSALM 118:17
I shall not die, but live,
And declare the works of the Lord.

TEMPTATION
(James 1:13-14; Ephesians 6:10-11; 1 John 4:4)

1 CORINTHIANS 10:12-13
Therefore let him who thinks he stands take heed lest he fall. No temptation has overtaken you except such as is common to man; but God is faithful, who will not allow you to be tempted beyond what you are able, but with the temptation will also make the way of escape, that you may be able to bear it.

HEBREWS 4:14-16
Seeing then that we have a great High Priest who has passed through the heavens, Jesus the Son of God, let us hold fast our confession. For we do not have a High Priest who cannot sympathize with our weaknesses, but was in all points tempted as we are, yet without sin. Let us therefore come boldly to the throne of grace, that we may obtain mercy and find grace to help in time of need.

TRIALS & PERSECUTIONS
(Isaiah 43:2; 2 Corinthians 1:3-4; 2 Corinthians 4:8-9)

1 PETER 4:12-13
Beloved, do not think it strange concerning the fiery trial which is to try you, as though some strange thing happened to you; but rejoice to the extent that you partake of Christ's sufferings, that when His glory is revealed, you may also be glad with exceeding joy.

MATTHEW 5:10-12
Blessed are those who are persecuted for righteousness' sake, For theirs is the kingdom of heaven.
"Blessed are you when they revile and persecute you, and say all kinds of evil against you falsely for My sake. Rejoice and be exceedingly glad, for great is your reward in heaven, for so they persecuted the prophets who were before you.

WEARINESS
(Galatians 6:9; Matthew 11:29-30; Isaiah 40:28)

MATTHEW 11:28
Come to Me, all you who labor and are heavy laden, and I will give you rest.

ISAIAH 40:31
But those who wait on the Lord
Shall renew their strength;
They shall mount up with wings like eagles,

They shall run and not be weary,
They shall walk and not faint.

WITCHCRAFT
(Leviticus 19:26; Leviticus 19:31; Deuteronomy 18:9-12)

DEUTERONOMY 18:10-11
There shall not be found among you anyone who makes his son or his daughter pass through the fire, or one who practices witchcraft, or a soothsayer, or one who interprets omens, or a sorcerer, or one who conjures spells, or a medium, or a spiritist, or one who calls up the dead.

EZEKIEL 13:9
My hand will be against the prophets who see false visions and utter lying divinations. They will not belong to the council of my people or be listed in the records of Israel, nor will they enter the land of Israel. Then you will know that I am the Sovereign Lord.

APPENDIX 1

WISDOM
(Job 28:28; Proverbs 14:8; Colossians 3:16; Proverbs 3:7)

JAMES 1:5
If any of you lacks wisdom, let him ask of God, who gives to all liberally and without reproach, and it will be given to him.

PROVERBS 9:10
The fear of the Lord is the beginning of wisdom, and the knowledge of the Holy One is understanding.

THE POWER IS IN YOUR VOICE

APPENDIX 2
PRAYERS

TABLE OF CONTENTS

PRAYERS FOR VARIOUS SITUATIONS............116

PRAYERS OF THE BIBLES..................121

FAMOUS PRAYERS................................124

PRAYERS FOR VARIOUS SITUATIONS

PRAYER OF SALVATION

Jesus, I believe You are God's only begotten Son, that You came down to earth in the flesh, died on the cross for all of my sins and rose from the dead on the third day, to give me eternal life. I now confess to You all of the wrong and sinful things I have ever done in my life. I ask You to forgive me and wash away all of my sins, by the blood that You shed for me on the cross. I now accept You as my personal Lord and Savior and ask You to come into my life and fill me with Your Holy Spirit. I love You and from this day forward, I will serve You and walk in the purpose and destiny You have for my life. In Jesus name, Amen.

DAILY MORNING PRAYER

Lord, I thank You for waking me up this morning and giving me another day to fulfill my God-given purpose and destiny. I ask You to fill me with Your Holy Spirit so my every thought and deed might be pleasing in Your sight. I bind, cancel and nullify every plan and plot satan has devised against me, my spouse, my children and my family in the name of Jesus and I thank You that no weapon formed against us shall be able to prosper. I love You Lord and give You all the praise, for it is because of You I can walk in victory today. In Jesus name, Amen.

PRAYER FOR FAVOR

Lord, Your word says in Psalms 5:12, 84:11 that You will bless the righteous with favor and that no good thing will You withhold from those who walk uprightly. I first want to thank You for the many times You have been gracious and merciful to me, by giving me favor in so many areas of my life, even when I did not deserve it. Today, if it is in Your perfect will for my life, I ask You to grant me favor _____ (name specifically the area, situation or person you need favor in). Thank You Lord for hearing my request and I claim favor in this area of my life, in the precious name of Jesus, Amen

PRAYER FOR PROTECTION OF CHILDREN

Lord, I thank You for giving us/me the precious gift of _____ (name of child). I thank You for encamping ministering angels of safety and protection to watch over this child today. I bind, break and cancel every scheme and plot the devil has prepared for my child today. I pray You will fill her/him with the Holy Spirit, so they may be able to discern what is right and wrong, holy and unholy. I pray that no weapon formed against them physically, mentally or spiritually shall be able to prosper and I thank You that You, who have begun a good work in them, shall be able to complete it. In Jesus name I pray, Amen.

PRAYER FOR DIVINE HEALING

Lord, I thank You and praise You for being Jehovah Rapha the God who heals. Your Word says in Isaiah 53:5, that by Your stripes we are healed. Therefore, in the name of Jesus, I come against the spirit of infirmity and call for this (name of illness) to be removed and for me/them to be completely healed in Jesus name. Father, I praise You that my/their body, mind and spirit is being restored back to their proper function, and I thank You for giving me/them the grace and strength to endure until my/their complete healing has manifested itself. In Jesus name I pray, Amen.

PRAYER FOR FORGIVENESS

Lord, Your Word says in 1 John 1:9 that if we confess our sins, You will be faithful and just to forgive them. I now humbly ask You to forgive me for (name of offense). Restore a right spirit within me and fill me with Your Holy Spirit, afresh and anew, that I may not commit the same sin again. Thank You for forgiving me and restoring my relationship with You. In Jesus name I pray, Amen.

APPENDIX 2

PRAYER FOR BREAKING GENERATIONAL CURSES

Lord, I confess to You all of the sins of my ancestors and predecessors. I repent, on their behalf and break, in the name of Jesus, every generational curse, stronghold and soul tie passed down or inherited. I thank You that Your Word says, He whom the son has set free is free indeed. I praise You for breaking past generational curses and ushering in generational blessings in my life and family. In Jesus name I pray, Amen.

PRAYER FOR FINANCES

Lord, I praise You for being Jehovah-Jireh, my provider. I thank You for how You have provided for me and my family all of our needs. I ask You to fill us with Your Holy Spirit, for us to continue to be good stewards of the finances You have given us. In Jesus name I pray, Amen

PRAYER BEFORE CONFRONTING AN INDIVIDUAL

Lord, Thank You for instructing and guiding us how to resolve problems we may have with another person. Father, I pray You will send Your Holy Spirit before me to prepare the heart of _____ (insert the name of the person you are going to confront). Give me the right spirit and words to speak, that will convey my sincere desire, not to offend this person in any way. Please help them to see the sincerity in my heart, as I desire to resolve this issue between us and bring glory to You. Help convict me of any area where I may be to blame in this situation. In Jesus name I pray, Amen.

PRAYER FOR THE PERSECUTED CHURCH

Lord, I want to thank You for the privilege of living in a country where religious freedom still exists. Help me to have a daily awareness of my Christian brothers and sisters, who are facing persecution and trials far greater than mine. I pray You would help them remain strong in their faith, and not deny You regardless of what the outcome may be. I also pray You will lay Your hand of grace upon them and protect their families. Touch the hearts of the government officials, as well as the citizens in that country, so they might see the testimony of these Godly Christians and by doing so, come to a saving knowledge of You. In Jesus name I pray, Amen.

PRAYER FOR BOLDNESS

Lord, I want to thank You for boldly standing up for me, by dying on the cross for my sins. I apologize for the times I didn't stand up for You, knowing I should have. Father, please fill me with Your Holy Spirit and grant me the boldness and wisdom, to know when and how to speak up. Let my words always be full of grace and seasoned with salt, so Your truth and righteousness may prevail. In Jesus name I pray, Amen.

PRAYERS OF THE BIBLE

PRAYER OF JABEZ
1 Chronicles 4:10

And Jabez called on the God of Israel saying,
"Oh, that You would bless me indeed,
and enlarge my territory,
that Your hand would be with me,
and that You would keep me from evil,
that I may not cause pain!"
So God granted him what he requested.

JUDEO-CHRISTIAN PRAYER BLESSING
Numbers 6:24-26 (NIV)

The LORD bless you and keep you;
The LORD make His face shine upon you,
And be gracious to you;
The LORD turn His face toward you,
And give you peace.

THE LORD'S PRAYER
Matthew 6:9-13 (NASB)

Our Father in heaven,
Hallowed be Your name.
Your kingdom come.
Your will be done
On earth as it is in heaven.
Give us day by day our daily bread.
And forgive us our debts,
As we also have forgiven our debtors.
And do not lead us into temptation,
But deliver us from evil.

DAVID'S PRAYER OF REPENTANCE
Psalm 51:1-17

Have mercy upon me, O God,
According to Your loving kindness;
According to the multitude of Your tender mercies,
Blot out my transgressions.
Wash me thoroughly from my iniquity,
And cleanse me from my sin.
For I acknowledge my transgressions,
And my sin is always before me.
Against You, You only, have I sinned,
And done this evil in Your sight—
That You may be found just when You speak,
And blameless when You judge.
Behold, I was brought forth in iniquity,
And in sin my mother conceived me.
Behold, You desire truth in the inward parts,

And in the hidden part You will make me to know wisdom.
Purge me with hyssop, and I shall be clean;
Wash me, and I shall be whiter than snow.
Make me hear joy and gladness,
That the bones You have broken may rejoice.
Hide Your face from my sins,
And blot out all my iniquities.
Create in me a clean heart, O God,
And renew a steadfast spirit within me.
Do not cast me away from Your presence,
And do not take Your Holy Spirit from me.
Restore to me the joy of Your salvation,
And uphold me by Your generous Spirit.
Then I will teach transgressors Your ways,
And sinners shall be converted to You.
Deliver me from the guilt of bloodshed, O God,
The God of my salvation,
And my tongue shall sing aloud of Your righteousness.
O Lord, open my lips,
And my mouth shall show forth Your praise.
For You do not desire sacrifice, or else I would give it;
You do not delight in burnt offering.
The sacrifices of God are a broken spirit,
A broken and a contrite heart—
These, O God, You will not despise.

FAMOUS PRAYERS

THE SERENITY PRAYER
by Reinhold Niebuhr

God grant me the serenity to accept the things I cannot change; courage to change the things I can; and wisdom to know the difference. Living one day at a time; Enjoying one moment at a time; Accepting hardships as the pathway to peace; Taking, as He did, this sinful world as it is, not as I would have it; Trusting that He will make all things right if I surrender to His Will; That I may be reasonably happy in this life and supremely happy with Him Forever in the next. Amen.

PEACE PRAYER OF ST FRANCIS

Lord, make me an instrument of your peace.
Where there is hatred, let me sow love.
Where there is injury, pardon.
Where there is doubt, faith.
Where there is despair, hope.
Where there is darkness, light.
Where there is sadness, joy.
O Divine Master,
grant that I may not so much seek to be consoled, as to console;
to be understood, as to understand;
to be loved, as to love.

For it is in giving that we receive.
It is in pardoning that we are pardoned,
and it is in dying that we are born to Eternal Life.
Amen.

PRAYER OF MOTHER TERESA

Dear Jesus,
Help us to spread your fragrance everywhere we go. Flood our souls with your spirit and life. Penetrate and possess our whole being so utterly that our lives may only be a radiance of yours. Shine through us and be so in us that every soul we come in contact with may feel your presence in our soul. Let them look up and see no longer us, but only Jesus. Stay with us and then we shall begin to shine as you shine, so to shine as to be light to others. The light, Oh Jesus, will be all from you. None of it will be ours. It will be you shining on others through us. Let us thus praise you in the way you love best by shining on those around us. Let us preach you without preaching, not by words, but by our example; by the catching force—the sympathetic influence of what we do, the evident fullness of the love our hearts bear to you. Amen.

PRAYER OF MARTIN LUTHER KING, JR.

We thank thee, O God, for the spiritual nature of man. We are in nature but we live above nature. Help us never to let anybody or any condition to pull us so low as to cause us to hate. Give us strength to love our enemies and to do good to those who despitefully use us and persecute us. We thank thee for thy Church, founded upon thy Word, that challenges us to do more than sing and pray, but go out and work as though the very answer to our prayers depended on us and not upon thee. Then, finally, help us to realize that man was created to shine like stars and live on through all eternity. Keep us, we pray, in perfect peace; help us to walk together, pray together, sing together, and live together until that day when all God's children, Black, White, Red, and Yellow will rejoice in our common band of humanity in the kingdom of our Lord and of our God, we pray. Amen.

A PRAYER FOR THE NATION
by Abraham Lincoln

Almighty God, Who has given us this good land for our heritage; We humbly beseech Thee that we may always prove ourselves a people mindful of Thy favor and glad to do Thy will. Bless our land with honorable ministry, sound learning, and pure manners. Save us from violence, discord, and confusion, from pride and arrogance, and from every evil way. Defend our liberties, and fashion into one united people, the multitude brought hither out of many kindreds and tongues. Endow with Thy spirit of wisdom those whom in Thy name we entrust the authority of government, that there may be justice and peace at home, and that through obedience to Thy law, we may show forth Thy praise among the nations of the earth. In time of prosperity fill our hearts with thankfulness, and in the day of trouble, suffer not our trust in Thee to fail; all of which we ask through Jesus Christ our Lord. Amen.

THE
POWER
IS IN
YOUR
VOICE

END NOTES

CHAPTER 1: WAKE UP

[1] Ira C. Lupu, F. Elwood and Eleanor Davis, "Religious Displays & The Courts," *The Pew Forum on Religion & Public Life,* June 2007, www.pewforum.org/uploadedfiles/Topics/Issues/Church-State_Law/religious-displays.pdf

[2] "House Office of the Chaplain- Staff Salaries," *Legistorm.* http://www.legistorm.com/office/House_Office_of_the_Chaplain/1531.html

[3] "Barry C. Black, Congressional Staffer- Salary Data," *Legistorm.* www.legistorm.com/person/Barry_C_Black/120.html

[4] "EPA Budget and Spending," *epa.gov.* July 12, 2012, www.epa.govplanandbudget/budget.html

[5] "Endangered Species Fact Sheets," U.S. Environmental Protection Agency, accessed September 10, 2012, http://www.epa.gov/oppfead1/endanger/factsheets.htm

[6] "Table 102. Abortions by Selected Characteristics: 1990-2007," *United States Census Bureau,* June 27, 2012, www.census.gov/compendia/statab/2012/tables/12s0102.pdf

[7] Obama, Barack H. "Robin Roberts ABC News Interview with President Obama." Good Morning America, May 9, 2012.

[8] "Teen Pregnancy." *Centers for Disease Control and Prevention.* N.p., April 5, 2011. Web. 18 Sep 2012. http://www.cdc.gov/Features/VitalSigns/TeenPregnancy/

[9] United States. The Public Policy Office of the National Coalition Against Domestic Violence. *Domestic Violence Facts.* Washington, D.C.: NCADV Public Policy Office, 2009. Web. http://www.ncadv.org/files/DomesticViolenceFactSheet(National).pdf.

[10] "2011 National Gang Threat Assessment—Emerging Trends." *The FBI: Federal Bureau of Investigation.* The Federal Bureau of Investigation, n.d. Web. 18 Sep 2012. http://www.fbi.gov/stats-services/publications/2011-national-gang-threat-assessment.

[11] "Hunger & Poverty Statistics." *Feeding America.* Feeding America, n.d. Web. 16 Dec 2012. http://www.feedingamerica.org/hunger-in-america/hunger-facts/hunger-and-poverty-statistics.aspx.

[12] "Abortion Statistics," National Right to Life, accessed September 10, 2012, http://www.nrlc.org/Factsheets/FS03_AbortionInTheUS.pdf

[13] "Table 1335. Marriage and Divorce Rates by Country: 1980-2008,"*United States Census Bureau,* 2011, http://www.census.gov/compendia/statab/2011/tables/11s1335.pdf

[14] "What celebrities think about relationships." *Glo.* MSN.com. Web. 13 Nov 2012. http://glo.msn.com/relationships/what-celebrities-think-about-relationships-7927.gallery

[15] "Sunday at 11: "The most segregated hour in this nation"."*God & Culture.* The Paul Edwards Program, 09 2010. Web. 29 Dec 2012. http://www.godandculture.com/blog/sunday-at-11-the-most-segregated-hour-in-this-nation.

CHAPTER 2: PREP UP

[1] Elliot, Elisabeth. Love Has a Price Tag . Ventura, CA: Regal Books, 2005. pp. 127-129.

CHAPTER 3: SPEAK UP

[1] "Abortion Statistics." American Life League. American Life League, 26 2012. Web. 29 Dec 2012. http://www.all.org/nav/index/heading/OQ/cat/MzQ/id/NjA3OQ/

[2] United States. US Department of States. Trafficking in Persons Report 2010. 2010. Web. http://www.state.gov/j/tip/rls/tiprpt/2010/

³ "William Wilberforce: antislavery politician." *Christian History*. Christianity Today, 08 2008. Web. 29 Dec 2012. http://www.christianitytoday.com/ch/131christians/activists/wilberforce.html?start=1

⁴ Sproul, R.C. Abortion: A Rational Look at an Emotional Issue. 1. Colorado Springs, CO: Navpress, 1990. 150-151.

⁵ "Rev. Dr. Martin Luther King, Jr. Quotes." Martin Luther King, Jr. Day of Service. Corporation for National and Community Service. Web. 29 Dec 2012. http://mlkday.gov/plan/library/communications/quotes.php

⁶ Fox, John. Foxes Book of Martyrs, Alachua, Florida: Bridge Logos, 2001. pp. 13-14

CONCLUSION: TELL HELL, NO
¹ "George Bennard, "The Old Rugged Cross" (1873), cited in, *The Baptist Hymnal,* p.93.

NOTES

NOTES

NOTES

NOTES

NOTES

NOTES